THE ANT

Delia del Carril, the Avant-Garde
Artist Who Married Pablo Neruda

Fernando Sáez

Translated by Jessica Sequeira

FICTION ADVOCATE
New York • San Francisco • Providence

A FICTION ADVOCATE BOOK

ISBN: 978-0-9994316-7-2

Cover design by Matt Tanner

Interior design and composition by Greg Johnson/Textbook Perfect

FICTION ADVOCATE
New York • San Francisco • Providence
fictionadvocate.com

Printed in the United States of America
1 3 5 7 9 0 8 6 4 2

*For my mother
and in memory of my grandmother
Julia Chaigneau.*

*Also as a Manual of Liberation
for my six sisters.*

Contents

Delia is the light from the window
open to truth, to the tree of honey,
and time passed without me knowing
if there remained from badly wounded years
only her radiance of intelligence,
the gentleness with which she accompanied
my pains, in difficult abiding.

—PABLO NERUDA, *Memorial de Isla Negra*

Prologue

To be born in Argentina at the end of the nineteenth century was to arrive in a place where the future was painted in rosy tones. To be born in Argentina, into a rich and well-to-do family, was to obtain all the benefits and privileges of a society that allowed for a comfortable life, free of setbacks, quite possibly happy.

In the case of a woman, these good omens were limited by the necessity of fulfilling certain precise and restrictive family obligations, and although a few breezes of emancipation had very faintly begun to make themselves felt, it was unthinkable that in the privileged, conservative and Catholic group of the Argentine oligarchy anyone would dare to deviate from the path of destiny.

Delia del Carril was born on the family estate in Polvaredas, in the Saladillo district of Buenos Aires province, on September 27, 1884. She was the fifth child of Víctor del Carril Domínguez and Julia Iraeta Iturriaga, who had thirteen living children out of a total eighteen births, at a time when the presence of midwives and clean water marked out the only difference between the births of the poor and the rich.

The Carril Iraeta siblings belonged to the third generation after the family reached its peak, a dangerous generation for many families, when decadence begins. This peak had been achieved by Don Salvador María del Carril, Delia's grandfather, who at twenty-two years old was already Governor of the Province of San Juan and afterward embarked on a remarkable political career.

But the arrival of the first member of the Carril family in Argentina goes back to the eighteenth century, when Carlos III, the King of Spain, sent Juan Vásquez del Carril y del Carril, born in a small bay on the coast of La Coruña called Camariñas, to be Royal Governing Mayor as well as Mayor of the First Vote in San Juan, a territory that in those years belonged to the General Military Government in Chile.

Don Juan Vásquez del Carril y del Carril married Doña Francisca Javiera de Salinas Quiroga y Sarmiento, and from their union ten children were born. The second son, Don Pedro Vásquez del Carril y Salinas, also Mayor and Governor of San Juan, a province that had already been incorporated into the Viceroyalty of the Río de la Plata, married María Clara de la Rosa y de la Torre. Of her twelve children, the fourth was Don Salvador María del Carril, Delia's grandfather.

Experts in genealogy have an unfortunate tendency to delight in ancestries, good marriages and coats of arms without worrying about constructing a truthful document that traces the ups and downs in old families' fates. They do not hesitate to leave ellipses and silences alongside names that might cast the lineage in doubt, fleeing from dark details and making the effort only to emphasize the attainment of lofty seats of honor. In consequence, the descendents of a past so heavy with eminent figures and exemplary lives often feel disinclined toward action.

After the independence of 1810, the Republic went through long years of political confrontation, a period of anarchy in search of a form of government that was could harmonize the interests between Buenos Aires and the provinces. With the idea of monarchy abandoned, the Unitarian and Federal parties were, in appearance, irreconcilable. And yet, linked by the intersections of family and finances, they continued to fight for the power to impose different formulas that could resolve the latent conflict.

In the midst of so many disagreements and shifts in policy, the Unitarian government under the presidency of Bernardino Rivadavia devolved into chaos. After a civil war, Juan Manuel de Rosas, Governor of the Province of Buenos Aires, would take control for nearly twenty years. Defeated by his opponents in 1852, he left the country without having found a solution. Over the ten years that followed, the provinces organized into the Argentine Confederation, which coexisted with the State of Buenos Aires without either proclaiming its total independence or joining the Confederation. It was an ambiguous situation, one that saw the beginning of a resolution after the war with the election in 1862 of Bartolomé Mitre and the unanimous acceptance of the constitution approved in 1853 by the Confederation. The dispute that had lasted for so many decades thus came to an end when the Argentine Republic unified around this foundational act. The political conflicts and quarrels went on until 1880, however, when under the presidency of Julio Roca, Buenos Aires was finally declared to be the capital of the nation. During these years the Indians were expelled from their lands, fifteen-thousand fertile leagues that when incorporated into the national territory became the origin of an economic boom based mainly on the exportation of grain and beef.

Throughout this entire long period, Don Salvador María del Carril played an active role on the second line of Argentine political life. A fervent Unitarian, he served in the Rivadavia government as Minister of Finance. The errors of the administration led to Rosas, his enemy, mockingly referring to him as "Doctor

Ingots", claiming that del Carril knew as much about economics as a man blind from birth knows about astronomy.

When the first Rosas government assumed power in 1829, Salvador María was harassed and forced to flee into exile with his brother, José María. They settled in Mercedes, in the north of Uruguay, making their house into a center of oppositional political activity. With all hope of returning to Argentina vanished, when the second Rosas government began, with an absolute mandate this time, the brothers opted to turn their eye to export deals with Brazil, just as they had done previously in San Juan.

Another one of the exiled families was headed by Don José Domínguez. After his death, he left his daughters a sizeable dowry, to be managed by the del Carril siblings. The guardianship turned to matrimony; in 1831 Salvador María wed Tiburcia Domínguez, and José María wed María Dolores.

Tiburcia Domínguez was seventeen, with musical and artistic inclinations, a friendly personality and great originality. Don Salvador María was thirty-two years old. According to a chronicle of the period, he was "tremendously serious, with round, lively, piercing eyes that bore into the soul of anyone with whom he was speaking, like a drill. He had a nose like Talleyrand's and a mouth with large thick lips, always a little pressed together, as if he didn't want to let secrets escape. All was symmetry and deliberation in this figure of noticeable height, who without towering was taller than the rest." Their matrimony wasn't unusual for this period when daughters often married a friend of their father.

Seven children were born, six sons and a daughter. The fourth child, Victor, was born on May 30, 1850 in the Brazilian province of Río Grande. This was Delia's father.

In February 1852, Rosas the dictator was defeated in the battle of Monte Caseros. This time, it was he who left for exile to England, and the exiles from his long reign returned to the country. Salvador María immediately became involved in politics, and was named Vice President of the Argentine Confederation, led by Justo José de Urquiza.

As constitutional Vice President and later Deputy, he actively participated in the long period of disagreement between the Provinces and Buenos Aires, which legally ended in 1862, when Bartolomé Mitre was chosen as President of the Argentine Republic.

The progress and enrichment of the country, which began in those years in fits and starts, did not leave Salvador María unaffected. At the time he already owned seventy-five thousand hectares in the province of Buenos Aires, including his Polvaredas Ranch in the Saladillo y La Porteña region of Lobos.

The family lived in Buenos Aires in a big house at 379 Moreno Street. Doña Tiburcia Domínguez enjoyed a prominent position in the neighborhood. With her great sympathy and generosity, she became an axis of social and cultural life, which thanks to economic prosperity, was growing more dazzling, less provincial. Doña Tiburcia stood out, above all, for being a colossal spender. Her excesses in the purchase of clothing, fripperies, ornaments, jewels and home furnishings, reached such levels that Don Salvador María, in complete seriousness, ran a prominently placed advertisement in the newspaper which said: "Salvador María del Carril does not take responsibility for any debts incurred by his wife, Doña Tiburcia Domínguez."

In 1870 Salvador María was named President of the Supreme Court, a position that he held until he retired in 1877. On January 10, 1883, he died of double pneumonia. His feats and achievements were recognized in the funeral rites. During the magnificent ceremony, Don José Benjamín Gorostiaga spoke in the name of the judiciary, as did Don Domingo Faustino Sarmiento, who with a certain exaggeration appropriate to the occasion, said: "To Del Carril we owe our existence as Argentines today."

As the owner of a powerful fortune, freed from the limits and restrictions that had been imposed by her husband, Doña Tiburcia started a new chapter in her high-rolling lifestyle.

She commissioned the sculptor Romaggioni from Italy to design and construct a family mausoleum, which was inaugurated in 1890 in Recoleta Cemetery. The top of the crypt has a figure of the god Cronus, and on the vault is a conspicuously positioned statue of Don Salvador María. On the door of the entrance, with her back to her husband, is a bust of Doña Tiburcia. It was placed this way at her explicit request, since she said she wasn't prepared to look him in the face forever. The liberation produced by her widowhood was such that according to legend, one day when she visited the cemetery to walk around the family tomb, she looked at the statue of Don Salvador María and said: "Now that you're up there, I can amuse myself."

The sober Spanish-style house at her ranch in La Porteña suffered through many transformations until it ended up as a French manor, and hosted splendid parties to which guests traveled from Buenos Aires in trains with sleeping coaches.

The big house on Moreno Street went back to its role as the center of an extremely active social life: dances, concerts, informal gatherings, poetry readings, welcome parties and goodbyes for distinguished foreigners. Now the grandchildren also participated in these events, benefiting from Mama Tiburcia's lavish splurges.

CHAPTER 1

1884–1889

In the southern winter of 1877, on the first of June, Víctor del Carril Domínguez, who had just turned twenty-seven years old, wed Julia Iraeta Iturriaga, who was fourteen. Neither the age of the bride nor the fact that she belonged to a family of recently arrived Basque immigrants formed an obstacle to matrimony.

The fourth child of Salvador María and Tiburcia had graduated as a lawyer, a profession he didn't practice, since he continued the family tradition of participating in politics. He became Vice Governor of the province of Buenos Aires and a National Deputy. He was also the administrator of his family's property near the ranch in Polvaredas, twenty-five thousand hectares of the best land, located one hundred and eighty kilometers from Buenos Aires, in the humid pampas.

Thanks to his dealings in the countryside, he went often to the nearby town of Azul, where he met Francisco Iraeta. Francisco Iraeta was a Basque trader widowed by Ignacia Iturriaga, who had died two years after arriving in Argentina, during the birth of their only daughter. Julia was sensitive to knowledge, with a special fondness for literature and music, and Francisco Iraeta had taken care to give her an education unusual for women of the time.

The new couple settled on the Polvaredas ranch, where they started what would grow to become quite a large family. Justa, Julia, Ema and Víctor had already entered the world when María Delia arrived on September 27, 1884. Later Raúl and Adelina, who would be Delia's favorite companions, would follow, and after them another six siblings: Conrado, Carlos, Mario, Emilio, Ofelia and Ramiro.

Childhood lingers forever as a secret time. From anecdote alone, it is difficult to puzzle out the events that can establish future memories, the formation of a way of seeing, the construction of desires and values, everything that makes up the elements that determine the rest of one's life. The happiness or sadness of an event cannot be understood to be merely happy or sad, for in these years, in a mysterious way, external laughter or tears can turn in a hidden inner direction, which is registered in a different, unknown way by the memory.

Delia's first years took place on the ranch. But the supposed freedom that one might assume from this fact finds its corrective in the strict discipline of schedules and customs imposed on the children, and above all in the clear differentiation between males and females. Too many prohibitions were placed on them all, but the list of obligations and physical demands was far longer for females. To be a man or a woman signified rigid, precise distinctions in education and behavior.

Discipline in the Carril Iraeta household was the responsibility of governesses, who corresponded exactly with their archetype

Delia with her brother Víctor at the Bosques de Palermo, Buenos Aires, around 1912.

as single, older, sorrowful foreign women—German, French, English—dedicated to the education of children from influential families in new countries, with a commitment to instilling good manners, languages, and primary school lessons, and also attempting to keep their pupils on the straight and narrow. The most serious punishments came at the request of the parents, who had both power and an iron hand.

As in every large family, discipline slackened as the new children arrived. Justa, the oldest of the girls, and Víctor, the oldest of the boys, received the heaviest burden. With Delia, who was the youngest of the older children and oldest of the younger ones, the demands were fewer, owing partly also to her own personality.

Life in the countryside may have given her a clear perception of freedom, but Delia also possessed an incorrigible curiosity and spontaneous liveliness, which didn't make it easy to exact obedience from her. Her first victims were the governesses. Against their authority, she waged an underground war in response to the subjugation of her older siblings, relying on the unquestioning loyalty of the younger ones, Adelina and Raúl. Delia was also her father's favorite, and his support placed her just a bit above the rules, allowing her to do what she pleased without thinking twice.

She quickly discovered that other and very different worlds existed, beyond the walls of the family house and the surrounding park. She was obliged to maintain a rigid distance from people who had entered the house to do work, which seemed absurd to her, and so she invented any pretense necessary to speak with them.

At four years old, her father gave her a horse—he climbed on and hit it with a riding crop, and Delia held tight as they galloped—so she could accompany him on outings in the countryside; maybe he intuited that going out, doing turns, moving around everywhere, was what most interested this wild daughter of his. Since she drew attention to herself with her strong will, he was forced to treat her differently, so her youthful insurrection wouldn't devolve into inevitable punishments that kept her in a state of permanent rebellion.

"If you want to kill yourself, why don't you throw yourself off the roof?" her mother said to her once at lunchtime, with everyone gathered. The older siblings didn't want to participate in Delia's crazy outings on horseback, doing turns, letting go of the saddle, galloping, racing as fast as possible. On stormy days, the sky was split in two by thunderclaps and lightning bolts, with a flash illuminating the trees of the park and water pouring over the rooftops. The storm's sound seemed to invite the children to race over the paths, but they could do no more than watch, hypnotized, through their windows, forbidden to go out by their governesses skeptical of the dangers such tremendous forces of nature were capable of unleashing. The governesses enforced these restrictions with a severity that resulted in beatings for anyone who disobeyed. But when the sunlight returned, with clear skies and transparent air, and when all that was left of the storm was broken branches, paths covered in mud, and deep puddles of dark water, the Fräulein or Madame could not refuse to climb into a carriage for an outing with the littlest ones. Meanwhile Delia and Raúl would go out on their horses, making them run in a stampede back and forth along the carriage path, splashing the governesses' recently-donned long velvet dresses with dirty water and mud. Delia and Raúl were always blamed for the mess. Delia, especially, for being the older one, for being a woman and for setting a bad example. Their discipliners insisted that the punishments were being doled out for their own good, so they wouldn't suffer from any accident. "If you want to kill yourself, why don't you throw yourself off the roof?" And Delia answered: "It is not my destiny."

Living in the countryside meant never knowing the routines of school. The governesses taught languages and proper behavior, and for more serious subjects, professors were hired who spent long spells at the house. Julia Iraeta also selected readings for her children out of the books that arrived from France, wrapped in thick layers of blue paper: books of poetry, stories and especially legends from Greek mythology that the children would sometimes discuss passionately with their father, in long conversations that left them with their eyes and imaginations turned to other worlds.

This world presented itself as too serious and too corseted, determined to break them down with its forms and manners. A girl had to groom herself, worry about clothing, not speak more than was necessary, sit up straight, eat with restraint during meals and lift the cutlery with delicacy. From morning to night, they were under the judgmental gaze of someone ordered to train them.

They found relief in games. Their ridiculous, noisy games with frenzied dances on chairs, wearing costumes and painting their faces with burnt cork, began as a parody of the world of adults, and were received with bursts of laughter and shouts. Delia remembered these as the best moments of her childhood. These amusements created a powerful affection between the siblings. They became a happy, inseparable group.

If Delia was the favorite of her father, who praised and protected her, she was the bane of her mother, who consider it unsuitable for a girl to have boundless energy or be in permanent movement. Delia's liveliness didn't seem feminine to her, and neither did her blithely warm, confident relationships with everyone around her. Delia scorned the example of her older siblings. But it was an unstable position. The freedom of life on the ranch was bound to confuse Delia and her younger siblings later on. At some point they'd be forced to acknowledge their position in society, and to respect the institutions on which it was founded.

Perhaps the children could be sent to Buenos Aires. But the unusual times allowed one to think on a larger scale. The countryside was producing a richness like never seen before. The humid pampa was surrendering great harvests of grain, which were beginning to be sold overseas; the flesh of animals was reaching the markets of Europe without difficulty, thanks to recent inventions that kept ships refrigerated. It seemed the right time to make the leap that other families in their situation had already made: a trip to Europe, to spend a long period of time to give their children an education far superior to what was available in Buenos Aires. In those days, it wasn't such an extravagant idea.

In 1892, the Carril Iraeta family began its first trip to Europe. Today it's hard to imagine what such a move meant. In addition to the family, which by now included ten children, there was a huge entourage, made up of servants, housemaids, governesses, countless trunks and provisions, chickens, and even two cows and their calves, so that neither eggs nor fresh milk would be lacking during the voyage across the Atlantic. The long trip began with the whole group in Polvaredas heading toward Buenos Aires in six horse-carriages, before they boarded a steamboat for almost a month until arriving at the port of Cherbourg. From there, they moved to Paris in two railway wagons, to settle at last into a hotel with two full floors reserved.

For the French, this influx of rich Argentine families did not go unnoticed, and newspapers spoke ironically of the customs of these new visitors, who spent a fortune to stay in the city for a few months, enjoying its opulence and adhering to an advanced culture that did not belong to them.

The children, however, were not overly impressed. Used to wide spaces, to a place of their own, they felt confined on these trips. The majority of their time in Paris was spent in convents where they were kept on as boarders. The del Carril girls stayed with the nuns of L'Assomption.

If the discipline of the governesses had seemed dreadful to Delia, the strictness of the nuns was unbearable. She rebelled against everything; she found the food to be particularly horrible. She could sit for hours in the dining room in front of a dish that grew cold without trying it, and the next day, the same dish with the same stale bread would be placed in front of her. Delia didn't give in; she preferred any punishment to giving in. The humiliations continued with religious lessons that preached self-abnegation and a list of the virtues that a young Catholic girl must display: submission, respect, obedience.

A return to the ranch became Delia's only consolation. What she had previously thought awful, she remembered as wonderful, for this other world now seemed to her a thousand times worse.

Delia recalled the periods in Madrid as having had more charm. There the del Carril sisters were interned with the nuns of Sacred Heart, where they took part in meetings and warm receptions whenever the nuns celebrated visits from the convent's benefactor, the wife of the Regent of Spain, Maria Christina of Austria, accompanied by her son, the future Alfonso XIII. From this period, a blurry family memory remains in which Ema or Delia faced the future king in a game of tennis, and because of something he said—a not very polite flirtatious remark, which at the time no woman, even less a South American, could accept— Ema or Delia, no one can quite remember, served him a slap with a big smile.

Eventually, owing to the political obligations of the children's father as Deputy of the National Congress and later Vice Governor of the Province of Buenos Aires, and because as they grew up they needed to start on a less disordered education and get used to life in the city, the family moved to Buenos Aires. The big house with two floors occupying an entire block at 3137 Santa Fe Street—with a garage featuring entry gates at Arenales and a service entrance at Billinghurst for staff and suppliers—became the new home of the Carril Iraeta family.

The periods at the ranch was reduced to summers. The annual return to those longed-for lands was marked by the arrival, at the beginning of the hot season, of numerous household staff, who proceeded to take down the drapes and roll up the carpets, stripping the big house at Santa Fe until autumn.

Julia Iraeta valued open-minded philosophical discussion and intellectual curiosity. As a result, she sent her daughters to the Italian nuns for education, rather than the traditional Sacred Heart school, where daughters of families of the creole oligarchy usually went.

The move to the city completely altered the children's way of life. Their days were filled with attendance at school, music classes, and meetings with cousins and friends, who gathered weekly at the house of Grandmama Tiburcia. The girls were expected to make an impression. To do so, they had to submit to long hairstyling sessions, select and purchase dresses, practice the piano and harp for many hours, memorize poems and attend singing classes. Justa was an expert on the harp, while Delia was an outstanding student of Aída Carvier, who considered her voice to be exceptional but looked to train it further.

In Buenos Aires there was no longer any forgiveness for bad behavior. The lessons in good manners had to be put into practice, widening the chasm between the masculine and feminine worlds. Delia challenged this injustice, leading to confrontations with her mother and with Justa, who rigorously followed protocol.

In heated arguments, Delia sometimes referred to her readings of the *Iliad*. She considered the Greeks to be deceitful and Paris a traitor, and she never completely forgave Helen for having let herself be kidnapped. From these readings she concluded that difference does not imply excuse, and that women have to take responsibility for their actions. So she was not prepared to submit to ridiculous social norms. These losing battles unleashed her instinct to be ever on the alert for a glimmer of opportunity when she could impose her logic and rationality.

Delia was not alone in these battles, and she continued to count on the support of her siblings, to whom she could now add cousins and new friends who visited the house. The Carril Iraeta family had become known for its joyous high spirits. Almost every day there were games, dances, choreographed ballets, musical performances, poetry recitals and "living portraits" in which literary works were represented, accompanied by famous musical pieces.

On September 19, 1898, when Delia was about to turn fourteen years old, her grandmother Tiburcia died. Her breast cancer had been incubating for a long time. In its obituary, the newspaper *La Nación* alluded to the youthful spirit the old lady had maintained to the last, and of course pointed to the success of the social gatherings she had hosted at her house, "providing all the pleasures of her hospitality without limit, and the charms of her graciousness that the years seemed to multiply." Her sixteen-year widowhood had not been spent in vain.

Although she wouldn't have liked it, she was buried in the mausoleum that she'd commissioned in Recoleta Cemetery, under the stone coffin with the remains of Don Salvador María, following a mass with her body on display at the Church of Our Lady of Pilar.

Víctor del Carril grew depressed after the death of Doña Tiburcia. Since his mother's illness had been announced, he'd been noticably sad. After her death he entered into a worrisome state of silence and isolation, imposing an extended period of mourning on his family that was only interrupted the following April, when they privately celebrated the marriage of Justa and Raúl Grondona. In the house on Santa Fe Street, the door to his room remained closed, and he demanded absolute silence.

With the passing of the years, Julia Iraeta's fears about Delia began to relax. Despite her tendency toward disorder and her inability to stay still for a single moment, Delia easily learned her lessons, grew interested in poetry, sang well and even—discon-certingly—worried to excess about her dresses and hairstyles.

On September 27, 1899, the day of Delia's fifteenth birthday, she was prepared to finish the mourning period for Mama Tiburcia. Her mother had promised her a big celebration to coincide with the end of a sad year. It would also be a recognition of her rebellious daughter's improved behavior.

On September 19, a year after Tiburcia Domínguez's death, mass was celebrated at ten o'clock in the morning at the church of Monserrat. Afterward, the heads of family went to lunch at the house of Victoriano Viale Ardinos and Julia del Carril Domín-guez, Doña Tiburcia's only daughter. Julia Iraeta had decided to go back to the house at Santa Fe with her children, arranging for Justa, her oldest daughter, to represent her during the post-funeral lunch, accompanying her father.

Before this lunch, Víctor unexpectedly took a walk in the garden. From the salon, the sound of a gunshot was heard. Some of the group went outside to see what had happened. Víctor del

Carril was lying in the grass, dead. There was no way to prevent his daughter Justa, who was pregnant, from seeing the blood and the hole left by the bullet in his right temple.

Víctor's death was the unforeseen end of a neurasthenia, according to the term used in the period, which designated all psychic illnesses. It had been aggravated by the death of his mother, and culminated in this decision on the day of its first anniversary.

The cause of death wasn't kept hidden. The next day, all the newspapers reported it, but only *El Nacional* described the event in detail. "Yesterday, with a shot from a revolver, Señor Víctor del Carril put an end to his days, after having played such a distinguished role in politics in the Province of Buenos Aires. Señor Víctor del Carril occupied the most crucial positions in the Province, for a brief time even forming part of the ruling government during the events of July 1893 that resulted in the transformation of the nation. Señor del Carril was highly prominent because of his status as a guarantor, and he had a markedly strong will and a firm measured pride. Ill for a long time, and convinced that a grave and hopeless misfortune was undermining his existence, he appeared to be taciturn and preoccupied, and withdrew from contact with friends who had always professed the greatest affection for him. This mood led to the terrible crisis whose outcome yesterday was suicide, as Señor del Carril was returning from a funeral ceremony dedicated to the memory of his mother. The event occurred at the house of Doctor Viale, brother-in-law of the victim."

Curiously, over the years, although the family never denied the event, they did change its circumstances. They began to claim that the suicide had taken place at night, in the house at Santa Fe, after Víctor had gone to the Poliatema Theater in the company of Justa to listen a performance of *The Sleepwalker* by the soprano Regina

Pacini, a Portuguese singer who would later marry Marcelo T. de Alvear. It was said that after returning from the theater and taking his usual stroll around the garden, he had shot himself as the desperate consummation of a neurasthenia that had persisted his entire life. It was as if the family wished to protect the memory of the deep relationship between Doña Tiburcia and her son.

In *La Nación* newspaper, the family announced another burial: "Víctor del Carril. Died on September 19, 1899. Julia I. del Carril, his wife, sons, siblings and the rest of his family invite their relations to accompany the remains of the deceased to the North Cemetery, on this day Wednesday the 21st, at 10:30 a.m. At the Church of Our Lady of Pilar, a mass will be given with the body present. Farewells will be made by card. The funeral home is at Santa Fe 3137. Note: Tribarne and Company will offer carriages until 9:15 a.m." That day, the flags of the public offices of Buenos Aires were kept at half-mast in honor of the deceased.

It isn't difficult to imagine how significant the loss of her father was for Delia. More than affection, a complicity had formed between them, a complicity that protected her since he seemed to understand, so much better than her mother did, her impulsive character, her outbursts, her real obsession with asking reasons for all the things that seemed out of place or unjust, and her stubborn insistence on doing what she thought seemed right, nearly always in opposition to whatever had been imposed upon her. But Delia never spoke of this loss, and the memory of her father was always linked with her first years on the ranch, with the horses and with his unconditional affection.

Feeling an urgent need for answers, Delia entered into a rapture of mystical Christianity, more in accordance with her thoughts and the pain of her loss than with a doctrinal Catholicism, even if she made use of its rites, attending mass every day at six in the morning and devotedly taking communion. In this way she avoided the feeling of emptiness, and opened the door to a lifetime of further searching.

CHAPTER 2

1890–1917

At thirty-six years old, with thirteen children—the youngest, Ramiro, was three years old—Julia Iraeta had became a widow. But she remained at the head of the family without falling apart. She was now the one responsible for the fortune that, in due time, she would share with her children, when they came of legal age. This fortune enabled her to make decisions with calm.

She handed over the Polvaredas ranch to administrators, hoping that her oldest children would eventually take control of their hereditary property. Feeling resistant to the closed society of Buenos Aires, she alternated family life in the home at Santa Fe with long periods in Paris accompanied by her single daughters. She acquired an apartment at 15 Rue Elysée Reclus, in an elegant neighborhood near the park at Champ de Mars and the brand new Eiffel Street, a perfect monument to the wealth of the industrial age.

Víctor and Raúl continued their studies in England, where they became famous not for their abilities as students but also for throwing extravagant parties and creating chaos. In drinking sprees, the del Carril brothers were unbeatable. In sports, if Raúl was winning a race, he would wait for Víctor, and they would reach the finishing line holding hands, long after the winners.

Julia Iraeta formed strong friendships in Paris, attending the literary salon of Madeleine Lemaire and the famous social gatherings of Madame Bulteau, where men of science, politicians and writers came together, behaving like characters from the past. Perhaps the greatest aspiration for a foreigner in Paris was to be able to attend these salons—the last bastions of a world in rapid transformation. Things were starting to happen in the streets, in cafés, at exhibition halls. Some were discovering the impressionist painters, while others considered them to be already out of fashion. It was a world quite different from the fledgling cultural life of Buenos Aires, and also from the one frequented by most Argentines in Paris.

The Carril Iraeta sisters had the opportunity, which they didn't squander, to read books that had been forbidden to them, and attend theatrical performances where they could catch a glimpse of the aesthetic changes in the arts that were beginning to demolish the principles of the last few hundred years.

The twentieth century had begun with auspicious and contradictory signs. Electric lights were livening up the nocturnal spectacle. With new elegance came a new freedom and widening of the social spectrum. Money was no longer confined to the aristocracy, and new socialist ideas reclaimed the rights of the working class. Small-scale revolutions took hold in the factories and mines, and they also found enthusiasts in the adherents of more unexpected professions, like the dressmakers and firefighters of Paris.

This social effervescence was experienced differently in Argentina. Although there were some rioters—like the students who shouted "Long live anarchy! Long live libertarian teaching!" in front of the Metropolitan Cathedral—no climate of agitation disturbed the creole oligarchy or the rapid progress of the country.

Women of the highest social class could participate in just one space: charity. Under the wing of the Catholic church, an infinite number of philanthropic associations emerged. These aimed to gather money for social works, and their members arranged parties, kermesses (festivals to raise money), dances and sporting competitions, which gave them the opportunity to make an impression and appear in the society pages. The Arch Confraternity of Our Lady of the Orchard, the Society for the Communities of Ill Children, the Society of Mercy in San Isidro, the Association for Poor Children of Nueva Pompeya, the Maternal Canteens, the Daughters of Mary from the Blessed Union, the Association of the Divine Image, the Brotherhood of Saint Vincent de Paul and the Society of the Ladies of Charity were some of the most conspicuous organizations to stir up social and artistic life with philanthropic ends.

"Only woman, with her intelligence, her activity, her altruism and her perseverance, can resolve among us the supreme problem of charity. The incessant working of the heart is united to the constant labor of the brain. There is no neighborhood in Buenos Aires, no population in the republic, that does not possess some feminine institution where the spiritual bread of science, literature and art is generously distributed in the most economical way possible," a magazine from the period opined.

Even here, Delia found a way to stand out. One day a lady of Italian descent, who had no invitation to the closed circle of the oligarchy, approached Delia with enough money to organize a fundraising event of her own. She wanted a grand ball, and she invited Delia to bring her debutante girlfriends, to help with the raffles, the sale of flowers and other small tasks. Delia told her that she could count on them. The official philanthropic societies, however, were not prepared to lose out that night to an Italian. They organized a big party at the salons of La Rural on the very same day and made Delia's girlfriends swear not to miss it. Delia saw a chance for transgression. When the day came, the party at La Rural had to make do with the presence of the young ladies, who went with Delia to her first commitment. The episode was referred to as the "Strike of the Debutantes."

Alternating between Paris and Buenos Aires gave Delia a sense of confusion that complicated her youth. Everything that had seemed possible in Paris—the freedom to think and act in a different way—clashed with the inflexible, absurd norms that had to be maintained in Buenos Aires, where any behavior that was not rooted in tradition provoked a scandal.

The house of the Carril Iraeta family drew criticism for being a focal point of modernity. The purchase of one of the new gramophones that sang and spoke as loudly as a human voice—sold by Cassels and Cía on Florida Street for twenty pesos—allowed the siblings and their closest friends to dance every afternoon to the rhythms in fashion. They also gathered to exchange books, recite literary texts and rehearse the latest scores brought from Paris. All this was fine, so long as it occurred in the house. But after the siblings went out riding on horseback through the forests of Palermo, a priest in a Monserrat church ranted from the pulpit against this immoral custom of the youths. Delia was unperturbed. "Nothing bad can happen when we're sitting in such an uncomfortable position," was her comment.

THE ANT

The two visions were so opposed, so incongruous with one another, that no path but open rebellion was possible.

In addition to her singing classes, Delia decided to register for courses in life drawing, line drawing and coloring at the Academy of Fine Arts, where the men and women gathered in separate rooms. She spent so many hours at the zoo, sketching animals, that she often arrived late to mealtimes.

In 1905, when Delia was twenty-one and her sister Ema was two years older, they debuted in society. Naturally, they didn't follow all the protocols. Before the season began, it was customary for a debutante to perform the spiritual exercises that would prepare her to enter society. The del Carril sisters considered this to be madness, and they flat out refused.

A detailed account of these exercises appeared in the social pages of *El Nacional:*

> Yesterday the prescribed spiritual exercises were practiced at the Chapel of the Sacred Heart by the young ladies belonging to the Association of the Daughters of Mary. We give their names as follows: Delfina Inés Clara Gallo, Carmen Vidal Martínez de Hoz, Carmen del Carril, Blanca Gómez Palacios, Mercedes Aguirre, Nieves Figueroa, Marta Lynch, Celia Cabral, María Gorostiaga, Clara Quesada, Josefina Roca and Lía Costa. Simply attired in dresses of dark colors, with their heads bowed down, they descended from their carriages in the early hours of the morning to lose themselves within the silent vault of the Sacred Heart. If someone indiscreet were to attempt to peak beneath the tulle covering their faces, he would see there reflected the ardent faith that dwells in their souls of pure virgins, and a languid, gentle smile visible on their rosy lips. It is the smile of satisfaction, of the tranquil conscience felt by those with no mission in the world but to be good and happy.

The chapel is cold and severe like all temples of God, and this is reflected in those pious souls, the Daughters of Mary. The day of forgetting the world has arrived for them, as they fervorously surrender themselves to the practices of sincere devotion necessary to achieve the pardon of the Almighty. Forgiveness in the form of phrases filled by evangelical dedication flows forth from the lips of the confessing father. There, kneeling on fluffy pillows that conceal the cold hard floor of the temple, as if they had been transported to a beatific region, they listen to the gentle and incisive word of this minister of God, who studies and analyzes social evils beyond any technique to combat them, comforts spirits by sketching examples of Christian humility, and teaches his listeners how to persevere on the path of good and virtue, to make themselves worthy of receiving glory. These eloquent talks elicit devout murmurs of approval from the virgins, and protests of repentance and perseverance. There they forget their father and mother, their siblings, their friends, and perhaps their betrothed, as they sacrifice the time claimed by their home, on behalf of charity for their fellow man, who begs with a sorrowful voice appealing to their sincere faith. And when the severe word of the speaker echoes in the shadowy vaults, they remain under the influence of a grandiose, eloquent mysticism that fills their souls, drawing them away from the positivism of the world, and stifling within them the idyllic nature of any promise of prosperity. When they penetrate into the Sacred Heart, they shed themselves of worldly vanities, outings, parties, theaters, horse riding contests, Palermo. Everything has been buried by a religious practice which imposes the necessity of attaining the forgiveness of sin, with repentance and the privation of all that flatters human weakness.

THE ANT

Go on, youths, for you have pure souls and still conserve the faith of children. Lay your sorrows, your beautiful weaknesses upon the blessed man hidden behind the mesh of a confessional, lost in the most remote corner of the church. Ask advice of him who at that moment, illuminated by the radiance of divine intelligence, will murmur into your ear sweet consolations and the pardon of God. You have spent three days at the foot of the altars. Your souls have borne, without giving way for a moment, the rigor of penitence, and have now been regenerated. Go out, enjoy the world once more. Enliven with your presence the places you visit, the streets, the salons. Your heads seem to be ringed by haloes of divine glory. Sweep luxury through your evenings, through the dance halls. Smile indifferently before the tortures of the helpless. Contemplate impassively, from your carriage pulled along by proud steeds, the beggar who implores at door after door. Because this is not a sin before the eyes of God. And if it were, then three days of seclusion, crying at the foot of the altar or on the prie-dieu of the confessional, would be enough to open the gates of heaven. Enjoy the pleasures that this world affords, for if you suffer a setback of fate, then God in his infinite goodness will stretch out a hand to preserve you from the disillusionment of the fall. You have the right to do so, for faith makes all things possible. Happy are you who still have it, happy are your future homes upon which the blessing of God will descend, as you grant to them your contributions of sincere faith and religious practice.

The debutante season took place over two busy months, June and July, and required its participants to dance almost every day, attend the opera and musical performances, preside over horse riding and athletic competitions, and serve as hosts at philanthropic events, all amidst a whirlwind of unrepeatable dresses and hairstyles. It put even the resistance of youth to the test.

That year, in 1905, the season began with a dance given by Señora Teodolina Fernández de Alvear in her home at 25 de Mayo Street, in honor of her granddaughters María Rosa Lezica, Josefina Lezica and Carmen Christofersen. Delia wore a Nile green empire dress with silver adornments, white chiffon, and pink Valencian embroidery on her neckline. Another memorable party was given by Enrique Green and Elena Napp Van Praet, in honor of their daughters and relatives, at their residence in Loreley at the top of the Barrancas de Belgrano. The house had an illuminated park and several salons, and in the hall a stage with curtains and drapes had been set up. As an orchestra played, the living portraits, or *tableaux vivant*, were exhibited, and the young ladies showed off their musical talents. Delia was in the chorus with Julia Valentina Bunge, María Calvo and Elena Green to accompany the portrait *Les Voix de Jeanne d'Arc*, singing Gounod's "Prière de Jeanne D'Arc". Cecilia Casares sang "Dit moi que tu m'aime", and *La gallina ciega* was accompanied by a Boccherini minuet. Later Delia performed in Saint-Saëns's "Egyptian" Concerto with Raúl del Carril, Julián Martínez, Lucrecia Bunge Guerrico and Mercedes Tornquist, who played the harp. The girls' dresses attracted attention. Each act was heavily applauded and had to be repeated, although the "Egyptian" Concert left the audience a little baffled.

They also went to see the equine duel of two famous horses, Pelayo and Floreal, at the Argentine Hippodrome. Pelayo triumphed by half a length. And they attended a party thrown by the Norwegian legation on Suipacha Street, which celebrated the coronation of King Haa Kon of Norway and Queen Maud, who wrote books under the pseudonym Graham Irving.

The opera season took place at the Politeama Theater—the Colón would be reinaugurated in 1908—and there were the debutantes again, listening to Wagner's *Valkyrie* featuring Longobardi and Talexis. They couldn't overcome the atmosphere of ennui resulting from the long lines of dialogue, but on other days they would enjoy lighter selections, such as *Cavalleria* and *Pagliacci*, or Massenet's *Manon*.

Delia, wearing white dresses of point d'esprit or pale blue muslin, a pink skirt with a dressing gown of white tulle or pompadour voile, or a white empire-style dress with golden adornments, made a new discovery: she had an attraction that made her different from other women. Maybe it was her open and spontaneous manner, which could be confused with lightness. Or maybe it was her way of laughing, her gaze, a certain distance. Whatever it was, she had it. Yet she felt a despondency growing within her. Although she had some very clear ideas, they all stumbled against reality. She didn't want to be a professional singer—that was a mad, frightening idea. But both painting and drawing required a great deal of dedication and time, and she couldn't decide. Her intense dissatisfaction needed an immediate solution.

She had reached adulthood. That meant an end to those great loves of adolescence, loves that occur only in the mind, loves in which nothing is said but everything suspected. For a young woman of her class, it was unthinkable to choose music or art as a profession—even in a liberal family, this would be too bold a step—and so her artistic pursuits dwindled into mere hobbies. Around this time, she received an inheritance from her father and grandmother. But her control of the money was purely hypothetical, since women didn't manage their own assets; her brothers or some administrator would do it for her. She would never inherit land, but only receive monthly dividends of the income. Delia's new financial independence didn't enable her to leave the family sphere. If anything was clear to her, it was that she had no use for matrimony: she simply wasn't interested in submitting forever to someone unknown to her, within the homogeneous Argentine aristocracy.

As Unitarians, the del Carril family belonged to the upper-class progressive bourgeoisie. They responded to the news of the priest who had attacked their rides at the Palermo park with a burst of laughter. The house at Santa Fe became a gathering place for young people who shared an openness to intellectual interests and Parisian culture, where they kept direct contact with innovations in art and literature. Years later, the group that had formed at the del Carril house would become highly important in the cultural life of Buenos Aires.

On Mondays the family gathered alone, without visitors. It had grown with the marriages of Delia's three older sisters, Justa, Julia and Ema, and her eldest brother, Víctor, who wed his second cousin Albertina Carabassa del Carril. These family gatherings were dedicated to performing chamber music.

During the rest of the week, Raúl and Delia received their friends. Ricardo and Manuel Güiraldes brought tango, the rhythm of the more marginal porteño neighborhoods, into the salon. As for classical music, the airs of modernity had saturated the group. They repudiated the usual preference for Mozart and the baroque, and chose Debussy, Ravel and Fauré as their favorites.

The sustained prosperity of Argentina turned Buenos Aires into a capital of the arts. In 1907 the new Coliseo theater was inaugurated with the opera *Iris* by Pietro Mascagni, interpreted by Enrico Caruso and Matilde de Lerma. Constant Coquelin's theater company brought the great actress Marguerite Moreno, and she would live in Buenos Aires for a time. Festivities were also already being prepared for the 1910 centenary, speeding up arrangements to reinaugurate the Colón Theater.

But Delia continued to search for something to define her life, as she shuttled back and forth between Buenos Aires and Paris. Only in the summers was her tranquility assured, when she returned to the Polvaredas ranch to gather with family and friends.

In 1909 she decided to stay for a longer season than usual in Paris, and sent a desperate letter to one of her older sisters:

I am in a period of darkness, my Julia. Sometimes I believe that I am a neurasthenic, but no, I'm not any imaginary patient. I feel that I don't have a reason to exist, that I don't live for anything, since I haven't even been able to save Raúl. I can't make anyone happy, not even myself, due to my inability to love anybody. You don't need me too much; at home I'm a nuisance. Darling, I don't want to tell you the depths of what I think, because it's awful. With this in my heart, you'll understand why I laugh at social success, why my irony degenerates into sarcasm. Lately I've been at parties hearing the kindest things in the world directed at my humble personality. They've declared me to be the most joyful, the most lively. And I've wanted to scream at them—idiots, idiots! Before arriving I cried, I sobbed, I shouted at home. I wish that these farcical comedies would end, they leave my nerves in a miserable state, and I swear that if it were up to me I'd accept Mama's threat to take me to Switzerland. At least I have the consolation of knowing how to sing, which makes me happy at my old age of twenty-five. Madame Trelat has come to know my voice, and she's got it into her head to make me sing before Gabriel Fauré and her old voice students. It's incredible. She's making me study some barbarity in Italian; it turns out she was a disciple of Rossini, and he has the oldest Italian school. I'm delighted, as you can imagine. I remember Aída well. If only I'd paid more attention and studied with her as I should have, think of everything I would have learned! Madame Trelat is severe and couldn't be more demanding, but she's very affectionate with me and gives me classes twice a week. Everyone congratulates me because they say that Madame Trelat must expect much of me, if she pays me such great attention. And her opinion is highly respected. But it'll be one more step in this useless life of mine without direction. Goodbye darling. Describe your boys for me, especially the third one, I don't know your nickname for him. Everyone tells me he's very adorable and looks like Ernestito. Hugs to Ernestito and a thousand hugs to Ernesto. May Ernestito and Martín not forget me, and may your third child love me. And for you, my Julia, all of your Delia.

This letter, in many respects contradictory, demonstrates the dual nature of Delia's situation. She had deliberately renounced the common path, yet didn't see any other options. She had to do something, but she didn't know what.

One of Julia's aims was to serve as a guide for her brother Raúl, the one she loved most, who was born right after her. There was no party or indiscretion in which Raúl did not participate. But Delia was only able to get him to return to Buenos Aires.

In those years, Delia was in Paris at the same time as Victoria Ocampo. They struck up a genuine friendship that, with its highs and lows, would last all their lives. Victoria was six years younger than Delia. They shared a critical gaze and many common interests that united them in rebellion. Victoria envied Delia's variety of events, her freedom. She had never been permitted these liberalities, as her family was much more conservative and had limited her outings, allowing her to attend only the events they chose. In Victoria, Delia found someone with whom she could share the details about the scandal at the Russian ballet premiere, when the dancer Vaslav Nijinsky, performing *L'après midi d'un faune* by Debussy with Diaghilev's company, had stunned the audience with the strong eroticism of his final scene. Victoria also admired her friend's self-assurance, her exquisite manner of behaving, smoking and dressing in the latest fashion, cutting her hair and painting her lips and eyes as if courting a scandal.

Delia knew very well how to conceal her inner disenchantment. Her double life of social success and inner anguish was the direct consequence of not finding anything solid in the superficial society that surrounded her. This failed encounter between her aspirations and reality left her feeling empty inside. She knew very well what it was that she didn't like, and society played at understanding her, but this was a long stretch from knowing what she truly wanted. Her friend Ricardo Güiraldes was in a similar situation, and they met frequently.

Two years younger than Delia, Ricardo shared a number of her pastimes and the same uncertainty about the future. With his good singing voice, he thought that his destiny might be music… or maybe painting, or even the writing that he'd practiced for years in secret. Many people believed that Delia and Ricardo were in love, but they were just close friends whose bond had been forged in Paris. Both possessed an innate charm, both were successful in society, and both distrusted their own charm and success.

Other friends rounded out this little group of Argentines in Paris: the sculptor Alberto Lagos, the brothers Oliverio and Alberto Girondo, and Alfredo González Garaño. They spent their nights chatting in the magical city, often along with the Catalan painter Anglada Camarasa.

In 1910 Halley's Comet heralded the end of the world. Nothing happened, of course. In Argentina, Ricardo's father Manuel Güiraldes, the Mayor of Buenos Aires, prepared festivities to commemorate the centenary of Independence. In Paris, Delia and Ricardo heard stories about the events. For example, Raúl del Carril had got himself involved in another scandal on the occasion of the visit of the Infanta Isabella, Princess of Asturias. He'd been chosen to participate in the retinue of the Princess, but bored, he'd gone to look for his lover at the time, a French woman he'd pulled from a brothel and settled into an apartment on Vicente López Street. Using his credentials, he took her to the Colón, to the official box seats, where her presence astonished the ladies. Men tended to celebrate Raúl for being an incorrigible playboy with abundant charm, but Delia got angry at him. She told him off for his inappropriate behavior in society and discrimination against women, but as always with her brother, she kept her criticisms discreet.

Then something happened with Delia's singing voice. It didn't emerge. Madame Trelat had asked her to sing in public, to show off her student's undeniable ability. But when the moment came, Delia remained mute. Her nerves had played tricks on her. Humiliated and proud, she threw everything overboard, and swore that she would never sing again. This episode convinced her to return to Buenos Aires. She didn't know what she would do there, but decided that she'd feel calmer in her own country.

The return didn't bring her much serenity. The administrators of her assets reported that her inheritance would soon become salt and water. She suspected that there had been some abuse. It irritated her that women couldn't control their own property, and that she was disadvantaged by the lack of a husband. She asked for advice from her brother-in-law Ernesto Vergara, Julia's husband, whom she trusted, but she didn't want to cause a family drama since other relatives were involved. Despite feeling incapable of facing administrative challenges, which had never really interested her, she felt afraid of losing the financial support that she had always enjoyed. The income from her properties was not enough. She hadn't been overspending, but neither was she prepared for any new and unfamiliar hardships. For a time, she felt herself to be living in poverty.

While everyone prepared their bags to get away from the suffocating summer, Delia stayed on in Buenos Aires. "Will the Ocampo girls be in Bristol? I don't know where to send my letters to Victoria," she wrote to Julia, who was summering with her family in Mar del Plata. She didn't manage to locate Victoria. Along with Lía Sansinena, Delia and Victoria had formed a sisterhood around the common desire for independence, as well as their indignation over the injustice of marriage, which they considered to be a kind of imposed slavery in which women were expected to tolerate everything without complaint. The eldest of them, Delia, was setting an example by resisting the obligation to marry.

The house at Santa Fe, too big and too expensive, was sold. Most of the family settled into buildings on San Martín Street or Paraguay Street, facing San Martín Plaza.

To pass the time, Delia returned to her painting and drawing classes. She felt that nobody took her seriously as an artist, and she kept her own desire to be one almost hidden, like an embarrassment. She'd take her papers and pencils to the zoo and come home with sketches of tigers, turtles, deer. Whatever she saw, she drew. Where is Delia? She's making animals, came the half-sarcastic reply of her brother-in-law Ernesto Vergara Biedma. What animals did you make today? Delia would laugh. "The devil will look out for me," was a phrase she constantly repeated.

Delia's lighthearted attitude might be confused with disinterest, as if she thought that everything was insubstantial. But this was her way of skipping over complications, of escaping a quagmire. Her whole personality could be summarized as being given to distraction. Delia lived in a rush of coming and going. Her distractedness grew more pronounced when things did not go the way that she thought they should.

Halfway through 1912, Ricardo Güiraldes returned from Paris after a long journey through Greece, Constantinople, Egypt, India, China and Japan. He'd been dragged into the adventure by his best friend Adán Diehl, whose keen intelligence and unfulfilled artistic impulses manifested themselves in his sharp criticism and avant-garde aesthetic. Ricardo came back with his head turned by incredible tales, fascinated by India and Buddhism, and serious about recuperating his inner life with a new religiosity that verged on mysticism. He felt the first symptoms of a deep change. When he returned to Buenos Aires, he was convinced of his true vocation as a writer, and carried drafts of three books which he hadn't had the time to edit.

Nor was this Delia's only friend undergoing a significant life change. Victoria had deserted her and got married. "This is madness," said Delia. But the bride was convinced that Luis Bernardo ("Monaco") Estrada, a rich, good-looking, cultured man she'd met many years before, could help her to escape from the prison of her family. He understood her interests and demanded nothing from her. On the day of the marriage she received an omen that made her afraid she was making a mistake: the groom's jacket smelled of mothballs.

The summer of 1913 would be the last one for the Carril family in Polvaredas. Complications with the many inheritors and their various needs forced them to make the decision to sell. To say goodbye to so many memories, they invited their friends over for a party. Delia brought Ricardo Güiraldes and his brother Manuel. This is how Adelina del Carril fell in love with Ricardo. She was twenty-four years old, beautiful, with big green eyes and a gentle personality, not at all intellectual. Everyone could tell she was smitten by the way she took pains to make sure that Ricardo had the tranquility he needed for his writing.

On June 2 they were engaged, and they married on October 20 at the Church of Our Lady of Mercy.

The newlyweds settled down in La Porteña, at the country house belonging to the Güiraldes. Adelina, so different from Delia, arrived at her new home with fourteen trunks that contained, in addition to all her clothes, several complete sets of sheets, multiple pillows and other creature comforts. In the peaceful countryside, with the support of his wife, Ricardo dedicated himself to correcting drafts of *El cencerro de cristal* [The Glass Cowbell] and *Cuentos de muerte y de sangre* [Stories of Death and Blood]. The wild bohemia of his recent years became the raw material for his works. In addition to her unconditional support, Adelina lent him her fortune, giving the writer a stability he'd never known. The Güiraldes were a traditional family, austere and well settled, but Ricardo didn't have a peso.

Delia, who still thought of marriage as something she needed to escape, felt more and more like a strange bird. Her friends had married in spite of sharing her beliefs. Was it a betrayal? At every wedding she confronted the same looks and same question: And you, when? It was one thing to belong to a distinctive family, quite another to distance oneself from the traditions that kept society intact.

At least no one dared claim that Delia was an old maid. Many men fell for her. No one could believe that all she wanted was a deep friendship, closer to siblinghood than love. Any time that she was seen with a male, they were assumed to be engaged. Delia continued to go out with friends and dance with married men at parties. She wanted relationships based on trust, faithfulness to ideas and projects in common.

Another one of Delia's friends, Alfredo González Garaño, also married in 1913. His wife, María Teresa ("Marietta") Ayerza, came from a conservative old Argentine family, scandalized by her marriage to Alfredo, whose nickname was "the Runt". The family knew he associated with artists, and feared that their daughter was entering a world of perversions. But Marietta quickly made friends with everyone, especially Delia and Adelina.

In June 1914, the assassination in Sarajevo of the Archduke of Austria Franz Ferdinand, inheritor to the crown, triggered the start of hostilities between factions that would eventually pit Germany, Austria-Hungary, Turkey and Bulgaria against England, France, Italy, Russia and Serbia. The First World War had broken out.

Delia's friends González Garaño and Marietta and Adán Diehl were on the island of Mallorca, having been invited there by the painter Anglada Camarasa. The war quickly brought them home.

Ricardo published his books in September 1915. *The Glass Cowbell* was a complete failure, so much so that it doomed his other book, *Stories of Death and Blood*. Neither the unconditional support of his closest friends, especially Victoria Ocampo and Delia, with whom he had always maintained an intimate friendship of visits and letters, nor that of his family, could free him from a period of bitterness and introspection in the solitude of the countryside. Adelina saved a few copies of the works he had decided to pull from circulation and throw into a well in La Porteña.

With the sorrows of war, Europe became a difficult place to live. Many intellectuals and artists looked for a way out. A good number of them turned toward Buenos Aires, which had transformed into the great city of Latin America, with an active cultural life.

In 1916, the well-known journalist José Ortega Munilla, along with his son, the philosopher José Ortega y Gasset, came to Buenos Aires to give a series of lectures. For Delia's group, who spoke to one another in French and whose cultural references began and ended in Paris, the arrival of the Ortegas was a complete surprise and a new stimulus. The philosopher was thirty-two years old and had just published his first book, but in Spain he was already considered to be a refreshing thinker. He had proclaimed that the old insular Spain was giving way to one that engaged more directly with Europe. The visit, which lasted for over four months, didn't play out in the usual official enclaves, but was organized by a small circle. Although Ortega lectured at the Faculty of Philosophy and Letters, he displayed the full spectacle of his intelligence at private gatherings. His thoughts, which would be collected in his next books, emphasized the necessity for each person to create his own authentic reality, defining himself through his creative actions.

The del Carril family introduced the Ortegas to their circle with a celebratory dinner at the Plaza Hotel which only the men attended, and with visits to their homes. The philosopher made great friends with Julia del Carril and Ernesto Vergara Biedma. They spent almost every day together, with outings to the racetrack and the theaters. Delia, who crossed pathes with José Ortega y Gasset many times, was amazed by his approach to life. He seemed to view it as a constant state of activity, of a movement between being and ceasing to be, due to the fleeting nature of our feelings. His thoughts helped her to organize her own, where before there had only been sparks and dispersed ideas. During one of these encounters, Ortega met Victoria Ocampo. Out of prejudice against the Spanish, she had not attended his lectures. By this time, she had already secretly decided to be an author, and did all her writing in French. But Ortega's fluid and perceptive conversations changed her feelings about the Spanish language and culture. Their friendship would last for years.

That same year, Isadora Duncan was presented at the Coliseo Theater. A true innovator of dance, she'd been accused by the Russian choreographers of lacking technique, but she dazzled in these performances, dressed in a light Greek tunic without adornments, in a program based on the music of Chopin and Tchaikovsky.

At the end of 1916, Alfredo González Garaño and Marietta convinced Ricardo and Adelina to go to Jamaica, since it was impossible to travel to Europe with the continuation of the war. Delia decided to join them. On December 30, they would take the train to Mendoza and from there to Santiago de Chile, and then to Valparaíso to board the ship that would take them to the island. That was the plan.

What hadn't been taken into consideration was that Adán Diehl would turn up at Retiro Station and insist that Delia marry him. The legend behind the story is that they'd agreed to see off their mutual friends at the station, and that the meeting between them was so transformative they decided to board the train, marry in Mendoza and finish the rest of the itinerary. But this is only a legend. Delia and Adán had met a few years before, when moving in the same Parisian circle. Adán was an alluring, cultured, tremendously intelligent man who knew painters, critiqued books and paintings, and occasionally posed as a poet. His family's fortune allowed him a disordered life of travels and adventures which he shared with his friends, all linked to the renewed cultural world that had sprung up between Paris and Buenos Aires.

Adán's attraction to Delia, four years older than him, was immediate. Used to getting his way, he had an anxious and hasty personality, and her persistent refusals only made him more obsessed. According to Delia, years later, it was the threat of Adán killing himself if she rejected him again that finally forced her to accept his proposal. This might be partly true. It's also true that Delia was thirty-two years old, with an uncertain future, and Adán was a handsome man with an unpredictable nature, a friend of her friends and so unlike the many other suitors she'd rejected.

What's certain is that Adán presented himself at Retiro Station by surprise and boarded the train with everyone else. They made the trip at night, crossing the pampa in the suffocating heat of the summer, and the next day in Mendoza they married without preamble. Adelina and Ricardo, and Marietta and Alfredo, served as witnesses. The announcement of the matrimony, sent by telegram to Buenos Aires and Mar del Plata, unleashed a scandal in both families. Nobody had a logical explanation for the event. The legend of a blazing love was born.

The newlyweds spent two days in Santiago before departing for Valparaíso to board the steamboat *Aysén*, headed for Jamaica. But they changed their plans and set out for a place where neither had ever been, sailing to New York, crossing the United States and Canada, and taking a new train, the Star, to Alaska. When their ship arrived in Panama—to cross the canal that had just been finished in 1914—the news was announced that the United States had declared war on Germany.

The strange decision to go to Alaska was typical of Adán's extravagance. In those years, Alaska was already a possession of the United States, hundreds of thousands of kilometers with only eighty thousand inhabitants, most of whom spoke Tlingit, and with enormous forests of conifers and animals prized for their pelts, such as martens, lynxes and otters. The gold fever that had transformed the Tanata Valley at the end of the century into an imaginary landscape of adventurers and legends had faded away, and it was taking on a new identity in tension between primordial nature and modernity.

Little by little, trains were replacing sleds in that immense land. Adán and Delia settled into a carriage lined with wood and illuminated with gas lighting. From there they appreciated the mysterious world through the window as they crossed the Yukon Plateau, penetrating the great forested mountains of pines and yellow firs where they caught glimpses of goats and bears. At times the landscape was so steep that the locomotive was hitched to the back of the train, to slow the descent.

Alone together, surrounded by astonishing views, Adán and Delia found serenity, but it did not last long. When the trip ended in May 1917, Europe was still at war. Russia, one of the allies, was experiencing a great convulsion, a revolution aggravated by the human and economic costs of the conflict, which in February put an end to the monarchy. With Tsar Nicholas II dethroned, the country entered into a kind of limbo that lasted until October, when Lenin established the first socialist government and Russia withdrew from the war.

Back from Alaska, to formalize their union, Delia and Adán traveled to Buenos Aires to the del Carril household, which still had not emerged from its astonishment at Delia's decision. She seemed to treat her marriage as almost a joke. Next they went to Mar del Plata, where the Diehls had a large house that they occupied year round. Adán's father was in delicate health, and his doctors had recommended a coastal climate.

Carlos Diehl and Isabel Laura Altgelt were an educated, refined couple, known as Papalito and Mamalita. Delia enchanted

Carlos Diehl immediately; he swore to be her unconditional ally whenever she required it. Adán's parents assumed that she would encourage him to settle down.

In this first year of matrimony, they lived in the Diehl family's home on Piedad Street in Buenos Aires. Delia had never been interested in domestic affairs. Arranging meals and disciplining the maids were not things that she had ever needed to do, and they weren't important to her. Nor did Diehl ask her to do them; it was a golden time in Buenos Aires, a city buzzing with activities in which to participate. Whenever they quarreled, they could turn to their friends—Adelina and Ricardo, the González Garaño couple—to reconnect and feel more sure of themselves.

Delia relationship with Adán was a passionate struggle that left no space for calm. They were similar in so many respects that neither would yield to the other in the long game of provocations, disputes and reconciliations. Delia didn't pretend to hide her beauty and charm. It amused her to make an impression, to please others; to her, coquettishness was as natural as breathing. These aggravations could get a rise out of her possessive husband, although he had his own charm with women. Their temperaments did not make things easy.

The shows that made the biggest splash in Buenos Aires that year were the ballets. Anna Pavlova, who had participated in Sergei Diaghilev's famous Russian ballets, had formed her own company and performed at the Coliseo Theater with *Coppélia*, *Giselle* and *Snowflakes*. But Diaghilev's company, which had already been to Buenos Aires in 1913, returned in 1917 to inaugurate the season at the Colón with its greatest star Nijinsky, in a revival of *L'après midi d'un faune*. This time the orchestra was directed by the young Ernest Ansermet, who years later, at the request of Victoria Ocampo, would direct the first symphonic orchestra in Argentina.

As artists, Delia and Adán were invited to meals and festivities with the ballet companies. Nijinsky expressed enthusiasm for a ballet that Ricardo Güiraldes and Alfredo González Garaño had worked on called *Caaporá*, based on a Guaraní legend. The text by Ricardo and sketches by "The Runt" delighted the dancer. They decided to entrust Stravinsky with the music, and to meet later in Switzerland to finalize the details of the setting. But the project failed when Nijinsky was diagnosed with schizophrenia and committed to a mental asylum.

The del Carril family continued their tradition of holding weekly gatherings at their house. The tango, which Ricardo Güiraldes had introduced to the salons of Paris, would always remain the dance of the masses in Argentina. But Delia's brother Conrado was a fanatic, and he hired musicians to liven up the weekly meetings. Around this time, the del Carril family took under its wing a young man, twenty years old, who would later become famous in the world of tango: Osvaldo Fresedo. Along with the brothers Raimundo and Domingo Petillo—who played piano and violin—Fresedo animated the evenings on Paraguay Street. He had started to play the accordian when he was fifteen, and he quickly developed an elegant style that was very much his own. From the del Carril house, he would go on to conquer upper-crust parties in Buenos Aires and Mar del Plata. Using his family's money, Conrado paid for return passages so that Fresedo and his orchestra could tour the United States. The musician remained grateful for years. Later, when he opened his own venue, "Rendez Vous," the revellers of the family were welcome for free, by invitation of the artist.

THE ANT

Delia and Adán continued to live between Buenos Aires and Mar del Plata that year. At the seaside, they became regulars at the Ocean Club and the Gold Club, fashionable places where they were viewed as an eccentric couple. Everyone had heard about the sudden marriage in Mendoza, and nobody could deny that they made an extraordinary pair. But the way they flaunted their charm and insolence seemed like a provocation to those with more ordinary lives.

A glance at the 1923 book *Veraneos marplatenses* [*Summer Holidays in Mar del Plata*], by Elvira Aldao, helps in understanding the revolutionary significance of Delia's behavior.

Now that these conversations in bathing suits have been introduced, it is to be feared that such lamentable nudism will become even more noticeable next season at the seaside, and extend to lunch and tea times, so that one can spend all hours of the day in a bathing suit, just as at the Lido, the famous Venetian beach where swimmers of both sexes mutually admire their sculpted beauty, giving it ratings in different categories. It must be hoped, despite it all, that this exoticism in poor taste does not find any environment favorable to its development, in the same way that cigarettes, less popular than the bathing suit, do not fit into our social medium. The environment is hostile to them, and the few married and single youths who have attempted to spread this masculine vice, contrary to femininity, have only managed to look like young ladies of the cabaret. On the other hand, the atmosphere has been only too favorable to making oneself up in public, that is, to adding elements to those that already appear on the face, which are not a few. This custom, ridiculous in the extreme, has spread in such a way that the most striking characteristic of all gatherings is the use of red lipstick and the white powder puff, applied before a tiny mirror to the lips and nose, with movements so similar to those of an ape that to watch them is to accept without debate the transformative theory of Darwin. Another imminent danger is the sacrifice of feminine hairstyles. It seems that the North American style of the bob has become stylish in Paris, which has exported it to the world. The Argentine woman's exaggerated submission to Parisian decrees will give no protection to her long hair. It will be cut as short as her ideas, going against Schopenhauer's maxim about woman. It must be repeated that the sale of these ape-like imitations of European extravagances, to refer to them in this way rather than as they deserve, has resulted in a general neglect of the culture of a woman's spirit, which is much more the case now in Europe than it was in our time.

CHAPTER 3

1918–1928

The horrors of war came to an end with the intervention of the United States and the defeat of Germany and the Central Powers. The painter from Paris who had settled in Mallorca, Hermenegildo Anglada Camarasa, had invited Delia and her friends for years to stay with him. At last they resolved to visit Europe.

Anglada had settled in Formentor Bay, a fabulous landscape of pine forests and transparent seas in the north of the island. The area consisted of a few stone houses without modern comforts, located on a small hill near the shore. The spectacle of the scenery, the solitude and the exceptional climate made up for the lack of luxury.

Daily life emanated from the Port de Pollença, behind the mountains that surrounded the bay. For bread and vegetables—and sometimes fish, if they couldn't catch their own—they went into town on a boat. Sometimes the milk would be turned to butter by the hurried journey of the boy who brought it in a clay jar pressed against his body.

It was a calm life, given charm by the fancies of Anglada, who proposed outings and excursions around the island. Occasionally they lodged in the houses of fishermen. At night they would take the boat to Pollença, for paella in the moonlight.

Anglada's paintings had nothing to do with the landscape. He prefered to ask his visitors to sit for portraits. He painted Marietta in an empire dress, and Adelina with a Spanish mantilla. Perhaps he also painted Delia, but no such portrait survives.

In secret, Delia was practicing her drawing. But she still had the shyness of someone who wasn't sure what she was doing, and Adán's harsh judgments didn't help. She turned to Anglada for advice.

After a few months in this paradise, they decided to leave for Paris. They settled into a big house with three floors on Rue de Saint-Simon, nearly at the corner of Saint-Germain Boulevard. The González Gavaño couple was about twenty blocks away, at 7 Rue Edmond Valentin. The war had come to an end, and Paris was alive again. Delia and Adán socialized intensely. Adán was always in search of new painters, and he was good friends with Paul Guillaume, who for the last few years had owned a gallery at Rue du Faubourg St. Honoré. It exhibited works by Derain, De Chirico and Modigliani, of whom González Garaño, also a great aficionado and collector, was an enthusiast. They went to the places in fashion among intellectuals, the Deux Magots Café and Lipp's Brewery, and on many afternoons, the bookshop of Adrienne Monnier at 7 Rue L'Odeon, where the authors of the moment, Jules Romains, André Gide, Léon-Paul Fargue and Valerie Larbaud, read fragments of their work for friends and clients. Sometimes musical programs with Erik Satie and Francis Poulenc were also included. That same year, nearby at 8 Dupuytren Street, Sylvia Beach would take the first steps to build her

Delia, Pablo and friends at La Coupole, Paris, 1937.

legendary Shakespeare and Company, with the help of Adrienne Monnier, an enthusiastic cultural host in a city that was remaking itself after so many bombs.

Other, more revolutionary art movements were gathering strength in Europe after the great war, movements in which this group of Argentines, delighted by the vibrant environment and its fever pitch of intellectualism, was uninterested. In Germany, Walter Gropius created the school of Bauhaus ("building house") which joined the work of architects, painters and sculptors into a single form that marked out a bold idea of the future. In Italy, after about ten years of struggle, the futurists, led by Filippo Tommasso Marinetti, managed to influence politics with an ideology of revolutionary patriotism, which was accepted by a new political wave that favored anticlericalism and antimoralism. And in Paris itself, Dadaism was exploding with the arrival of Tristan Tzara from Zurich. André Breton and Louis Aragon, new editors of the magazine *Littérature*, joined him, before they distanced themselves five years later to found the surrealist movement.

In the daily life of the Diehl marriage, the constant personality clashes, as well as Adán's jealousy and abrupt changes of character, started to make their life together feel like an inferno. Delia was restricted from going out. If she wanted to take painting classes, she had to do so in the enormous house where they lived, under no circumstances at an academy, let alone in the studio of a painter. She wasn't easy to subdue, and she entered into battle for her freedom. The verbal fights turned into colossal rows. Plates and vases flew. It would seem that the attraction between them required such arguments. Adán's erratic behavior showed Delia there was something more than an eccentric and complicated personality at play. Drugs were a pastime he had acquired during his bachelor period, on his multiple travels. He'd tried everything, but morphine had become a habit. Their differences deepened, the violence of their reactions multiplied. In desperation, Adán would come to wake her when she was sleeping, to ask her who was appearing in her dreams. His jealousy was an obsession, even though he was the unfaithful one.

Delia was still courted as if she were a single woman. To her it seemed very amusing. But she feared violence, and many times she accompanied Adán on his artificial flights so that he would feel her by his side as a suitable companion, an accomplice. As a couple they were still united by their education, a mutual respect and good manners. There was also a certain degree of admiration, which showed itself in their judgments on readings or works of art. They were two clever dilettantes, curious, with the bitter taste of frustration that secretly made them understand one another. They attempted to limit their controversies to private life. But as living together grew more difficult, Delia embarked on a period of tremendous agitation.

Adelina and Ricardo arrived in August 1919, settling in with them on the third floor of the house on Rue de Saint-Simon, and relieving the tension at a crucial moment.

Ricardo had recovered from his failures with a six-hundred page draft of *Xaimaca*, inspired by the trip that he had taken, a draft reduced to a little over a hundred pages upon publication. He gave the mystical poems that he had composed during his previous rural retreat to Delia and Adán to read.

Delia was very enteratined by Adelina's change of personality. She had arrived, predictably, with many trunks containing all her household items. What was new was her way of treating Ricardo. Fearing that, through his friendship with Adán, Ricardo would return to a life of adventure, she insisted on schedules and discipline. The writer accepted his subjugation with good humor, and said that from then on they would be called Ricarda and Adelino.

The González Garaño couple planned to leave for vacation in Pollença and bring the Güiraldes couple with them. Adán decided that they would instead return to Argentina, as his father was in poor health. This was also an excuse to avoid the trip with the group.

In Mar del Plata, Delia dedicated herself to taking care of her father-in-law. The truth is that she found refuge under the wing of Adán's family, which understood the couple's conflicts, and felt affection toward her.

As in so many cases, inertia postponed any definite decision about the unstable marriage. Adán's father died after a long illness. Now was not the time for Delia to pull away from her husband. They went again to Paris. Adelina and Ricardo were still there, enthusiastic about their new friends like the writer Valéry Larbaud, whom Güiraldes had arranged to meet after admiring his novel *Barnabooth*, which Adán had recommended. Social gatherings at the bookstore of Adrienne Monnier opened unexpected doors, enabling him to meet and live alongside the writers of the moment.

At Diehl's insistence, they all went again that summer to Mallorca. After the death of his father, he had inherited a fortune, and he thought he might pursue his idea to buy an enormous plot of land on the island, and build a place to shelter artist friends from all over Europe.

Mallorca was still magical. During the day they swam in its crystal-clear waters, walked, and climbed hills, and at night they sailed in a little boat with a carbide lantern at the prow that illuminated the sea, in search of the squid and octopus fishermen.

Anglada Camarasa continued to invent new settings. The group had expanded with the presence of the painters Tito Cittadini, who was an old friend, and Gregorio López Naguil, who was married to a girl from Pollença. The González Garaño couple had built their own house, and they kept a guest room for Delia and Adán.

Adelina and Ricardo, enthusiastic about the landscape, rented a house there themselves for three years. Adán started negotiations to buy the thousands of hectares at Formentor that for two centuries had remained in the hands of a single family, the Costas. He was not intimidated by the difficulty—even if it took years, he would achieve it.

What ended the marriage was not the great fights, the broken plates, the vases smashed to shards against the wall, the pitched battles with hand raised countless times, the endless scenes of Adán's jealousy, or the complexities of two strong personalities. It is possible that all these challenges provided fuel for a delirious relationship that offered secret mutual advantages. But when Delia found out about her husband's tempestuous love for a well-known Spanish dancer who was all the rage in Paris, she found the perfect justification to leave him immediately, without waiting for contractual arrangements, much less economic compensation. She only took the time to destroy all the drawings and paintings that had accumulated in the workshop, her sole personal refuge.

She returned to Argentina on the *Massilia*, a boat that set sail toward Buenos Aires from the port of Vigo in the first days of January 1921. The marriage had lasted for four years, too long for Delia, whose nerves were ruined. She thought it would be difficult to recover the happiness and ease that had characterized her earlier life. The recent past felt like a nightmare. Once again the company of friends—Ricardo and Adelina and the González Garaño couple made the long steamboat journey with her—was better than anything in the world, as they had lived through everything near her, and could understand.

Especially Ricardo, who was coming back from several experiences similar to hers. After his literary failures, he had returned to his origin: to nature, to the countryside where he found peace far from the clamor of society, and to the shelter and spiritual healing he had found in his passage through India, which had showed him the path to writing. Delia did not have the tools that Ricardo did, only the impulse to do something artistic. So far this hadn't crystallized, and she didn't feel that she was fully accepted by the others. Delia was always a necessary character, essential to her friends, one who livened things up, excelled at improvisation, showed interest in everything and had a curious way of drawing on many ideas to form an attractive conversation. But she ended up treating these abilities as a joke, stripping them of their importance so her friends wouldn't take her seriously. It was a dangerous game, one that left her feeling resentful and alone.

After a few days in Buenos Aires, in order to escape the damp heavy summer, she went with Ricardo and Adelina to Dos Talas, a ranch belonging to the Sansinena family. Lía was there, her life-long friend, at whose house, years before, she had attended so many parties and performances, including the famous living portraits. Delia, older than the rest of the group, had always enjoyed adding a comic and farcical note to relax the nerves of the actresses and singers. She'd never taken herself seriously, and perhaps this is how she preferred it.

The countryside, the outings on horseback, the tranquility made her consider her situation with greater calm. She needed to reinvent her life.

Back in Buenos Aires, she settled into an apartment on Paraguay Street. Unconcerned with domestic affairs, she decided to innovate by bringing in cushions to receive her friends, without complicating things with furniture. Furniture didn't interest her; it wasn't necessary, except for a grand piano, on which she continued to practice although she had cast away singing forever.

Delia's mother kept silent about the separation. Her closest siblings, Julia and Raúl, who knew Adán well, admitted that this conclusion was inevitable. The rest saw it as another mad decision by Delia. But she didn't give explanations, and didn't think she had to change her way of living or shut herself away forever because of the disaster. She started again in Buenos Aires, a city that in many respects had abandoned its provincial atmosphere. Cultural movements were beginning to appear within small groups, encouraged by the fierce winds of modernity blowing from Europe. She was like a fish in water with these people. Victoria Ocampo, whom she had now begun to meet again, admired her for her bravery. She had been living for eight years under the same roof as Monaco Estrada, who had never understood her, and it was an open secret that she had taken a lover, Julián Martínez, her husband's cousin, with whom she maintained a clandestine relationship. Victoria was afraid of her family, and with good reason, since they had created a scandal after her works as a writer began to appear in the newspaper *La Nación*. But the following year Victoria decided to separate, and went to live alone in an apartment on Montevideo Street.

The situation was complicated for these women. They had to operate in the disguise of what they wanted to be, taking steps forward and steps back, in a balance that was difficult to maintain, to avoiding the front line, acting with delicacy so as not to be rejected in a society controlled by men; avoiding taking stands so as not to be excluded from their families; avoiding plunging headlong into new worlds so as not to be seen as pretentious upstarts. The only thing that protected them was their economic independence, a security that Delia never boasted about, but that gave her the support and permission to move about with ease. Emancipation was only possible for them on the basis of this other freedom.

Through letters from Larbaud to Ricardo, Delia had news of Adán, of his new trips to Tunisia and Mallorca and of the translations he was making into Spanish of this writer's work *Enfantines*. She didn't want to know any more. She was afraid to meet him again in Argentina, and the news that he was abroad calmed her.

She resumed her painting classes, which seemed to soothe her anxiety about not having an avenue for her artistic searching. Friendships and daily outings recomposed her spirits.

In those first years of the '20s, writers and poets began to form groups, write manifestos and found cultural magazines like *Proa*, *Martín Fierro* and *Prisma*, whose large-format sheets featured both writing and art. Like all publications of this kind, they appeared, disappeared and emerged again, forming chapels that raised different banners, some more devoted to aesthetics, others more political, but all prepared to sweep away the old visions, as they clamored for an openness to new forms of art and modernity.

The poet Oliverio Girondo was one of the fiercest members of the avant-garde, the most opposed to the old Argentine cultural world. He was, like Delia's group of friends, very cosmopolitan, and a friend to many French writers such as Blaise Cendrars and Paul Morand. His book *Veinte poemas para ser leídos en el tranvía* [Poems to Read on a Streetcar], published in 1922, is full of irony and humor, weapons that can reveal human foolishness and the stupidity of social and religious conventions. He and Jorge Luis Borges had returned from Spain, influenced by Ultraism, the movement on the peninsula that assimilated French symbolism to reject conventional poetry and champion free verse. But Girondo went further, putting sex on the table, abjuring all types of morality founded on virginity and matrimony, mocking the Catholic church and its conventions and calling for transgression as the only vehicle toward the modern.

As always in history, similar movements were taking place at the same time. In Madrid, a group of students invented the disparaging term "Putrefactos" to call out those who had settled into stagnation, continuing their outmoded practices and snubbing the rejuvenated airs of modernity. Federico García Lorca, Luis Buñuel, Salvador Dalí and Pepín Bello were the young people who invented and spread this word, which became a sensation in intellectual publications.

Nobody remains to confirm the rumor spread by some about the love affair of Delia with Oliverio Girondo, an intense and brief relationship that led to a long friendship. If it happened, it was likely in 1924, the year when all this intellectual commotion began to take on more concrete forms.

Delia had spent the summer in La Porteña, at the ranch of the Güiraldes couple, dedicating herself to her favorite pastimes of riding on horseback like a man, painting the wood panels she shared with Ricardo, engaging in conversation, showing off her charms, and, even now, scandalizing visitors, as she smoked like a convict and walked around all day long in her riding outfit of breeches and boots. All these forbidden things she flaunted with insolence, as if they were perfectly natural.

In February the first issue of the magazine *Martín Fierro* appeared, directed by a poet from Córdoba, Evar Méndez, with the support of Oliverio Girondo, who was the true intellectual driving force behind the publication. From the start the magazine had a political aspect, attacking the Pope, the Catholic Church and the Tsarist ambassador from Russia who, despite the October revolution of 1917, still continued his activity in Argentina. It attacked all obsolete authority, and of course, the poets of the old guard.

Girondo called for the solidarity of writers and the creation of a United Front, forcing Ricardo Güiraldes to emerge from his reclusion and participate. The exchange between the writers grew more intense. Ricardo met Borges, fascinated by his book *Fervor of Buenos Aires*, as well as other poets like Raúl González Tuñón who came from different spheres in Buenos Aires, more marginal and politically committed. Güiraldes encouraged him to widen their world to writers who had not had the luck, like himself, Borges and Girondo, of having met the poets of Europe on their travels. Rimbaud, Lautréamont, Saint-John Perse and his friend Valéry Larbaud were introduced during meetings at the Majestic

Hotel, where Ricardo lived when he came back from La Porteña. Adelina and Delia were the only women in the group.

That year Amigos del Arte was inaugurated as well, with the presidency of Elena (Bebé) Sansinena de Elizalde and the support of the artist "the Runt" González Garaño. This space was without a doubt more aristocratic and less abuzz with reformist initiatives than the writers' space, but it also fulfilled the role of being a fundamental part of the cultural life in those years. Painters, philosophers, musicians and theater people who appeared in Buenos Aires gave talks. Of course Delia, Ricardo and Adelina also played a role, helping out their old friends in the organization.

The meeting between Güiraldes and Borges, arranged by another poet, Brandan Caraffa, with the participation of Pablo Rojas Paz, resulted in the creation of the magazine *Proa*, which published its first issue in August 1924. *Proa* became the major literary magazine of the moment, giving a meticulous account of new approaches to writing original prose and poetry, with a more scandalous exuberance than *Martín Fierro*, although the two magazines shared many contributors.

Apart from the literary groups, Delia's social life revolved around Pedro Figari, the Uruguayan painter. One of his greatest collectors was Ricardo's father, who had sold his collection of nineteenth-century paintings to replace them with magnificent works on cardboard made by the new artist. The other great collector was Victoria. She received the writers and artists of the moment at her house without actively participating in any of the groups, more concerned with her own endeavors, like a monograph on Dante called "From Francesca to Beatrice" published in *Revista de Occidente*, directed in Spain by José Ortega y Gasset.

Güiraldes noted in his diary multiple lunches and meals with Delia, where they commented on exhibitions, talks, readings and critical essays. These snippets of conversation traced a bond between them.

In the atmosphere of these emerging artists and cultural movements that laid the foundation for the following decades, Delia and her liveliness played an important role. She knew everybody, she came and went freely, she helped to organize events, she was loved and sought after; but this wasn't enough for her. Although she was intelligent enough to absorb knowledge and make impressive conversation, there was still something she lacked, something solid that could properly position her. Eternally pursuing her was the specter of banality, a fashionable word that was often heard on the lips of others, referring to women like her who circulated through prohibited spaces and abandoned the rules of society. The word was an unbearable provocation and a stain on one's reputation.

Whatever happened and wherever she participated, she was always driven by intense doubts and anxieties. This anguish formed an obstacle to her self-discovery, as it didn't allow her the calm required to probe the depths of her being, and spurred her toward inner evasions.

With a group of her siblings and nephews she went to spend the summer at the ranch of the Peralta Alvear couple, at the invitation of her brother Carlos, who was married to Susana Peralta Alvear.

During a duck shoot when Conrado, another brother of Delia's, was teaching his nephew Raúl Grondona, the son of Justa del Carril, how to use a shotgun, the boy aimed at a duck that swooped out of sight before the shot. "Here's another!" his uncle shouted. As Raúl turned in search of the new target, a bullet emerged that hit Conrado in the neck, crossing through his carotid artery. After sending a goodbye kiss to his mother, he died almost instantly. Conrado was single, a sailor, thirty-four years old.

The witnesses to the accident avoided any judicial problems that might have followed the tragedy, but the family was devastated. Justa's son hid his involvement from her to avoid further pain, preventing her from reading the newspapers that reported the event. The previous year her husband had died of a heart attack, and she had given birth to a stillborn son. A few months later, a woman who came to do her nails at the apartment made a kind comment about the suffering she must be facing becaues of her oldest son having killed her brother Conrado. That is how she found out.

Justa's tragedies seemed to have no end. It was she who found their father on the day of his suicide. Her older son had now been dealt his misfortune; the next tragedy came for her younger one, born three months after the death of her husband. When he was seven years old, he visited the Savoy Hotel, where his Bosch Grondona cousins from Spain were staying for his first communion. While playing with a cousin his age, under mysterious circumstances, both fell from a large open window, crashing through a skylight that shattered into a thousand pieces. Their bodies landed in the hallway of the hotel. Justa's son died instantly. His cousin survived for two months. Justa reacted to this tremendous blow by shutting herself away in her apartment on Santa Fe and Callao, without going out except to her country house in Radinach for the summer.

But the tragedies continued. Years later, another one of her sons, Jorge, arranged what was in her eyes a bad marriage, and she couldn't tolerate the situation. She was a strict, demanding adherent to norms, and she acted like an old-world aristocrat. Adelina, who gave a nickname to everyone, had two for her:

"Queen Conga" and "The English Lady." Jorge died of tuberculosis seven months after the marriage. Raúl, the favorite son, gave
her a grandson, her only one, who died of meningitis a year and
a half after he was born. Her other son, Alberto, was burned alive
after his car caught fire following a marriage reception at a ranch
in Monte Grande. Her only daughter, Nenona, remained a spin-
ster. Some in the family claimed that it was the tragedies, the fear
of such fatalities, that had scared away any possible fiancés.

While the death of Conrado diminished the joy and opti-
mism of the del Carril family, Julia's death from cancer, in June
of that same year, came as another crushing blow. Julia, Delia's
sister, had been an irreplaceable friend and confidant. In her
honor Delia made a vow to the Virgin of Luján one night as she
walked in the company of Jorge Luis Borges, another skeptic.
"When someone beloved is dying, one is capable of believing in
anything," Delia said.

The sadness of these deaths profoundly changed her. Faced
with such incomprehensible realities, her illusion of happiness,
and her sense of forward movement in a life of detached ease,
seemed to collapse. She saw these events as punishment for her
vanity, for those privileges that she had believed to be natural
merits, and she felt a powerful call to turn an appreciative gaze
on life. "I decided to be immortal, I wanted to be immortal," she
remembered long afterward.

But the family was made of sturdy material. Julia Iraeta, their
mother, bore the losses without complaint, and without words,
with the courage of her severe Basque heritage. Through her
example, Delia discovered this trait in herself, too.

The time of sadness didn't end there. After the appearance
of *Don Segundo Sombra* in July 1926, for which he received his
first sincere congratulations from friends and open recognition

for a writing career he had doubted, Ricardo Güiraldes suffered from a new relapse. The illness would fade away, only to come back even worse.

Güiraldes, long admired for his physical appearance, declined steadily as the sickness came and went, lying in wait, eating away at him. His teeth fell out and he grew a mustache to cover it up, while the dentist prepared a replacement. Adelina hated the mustache. Without considering his own suffering, she put curlers into her hair and walked around in them all day long, which he couldn't bear. She didn't tell him to cut off his moustache, but she did say that if he was able to do what he liked, then she had an equal right. No doubt it was Adelina who brought order to his bohemian life. Ricardo, write; Ricardo, it's time to rest; Ricardo, don't drink coffee—something that he liked but had been forbidden. These were Adelina's constant refrains. As his nephews tell it, Adelina adored Ricardo, she cried over him for the rest of her life, but while he was alive she drove him crazy.

When the illness got worse, they left for Paris in the hopes of continuing their travels to India. In his last years, Ricardo's readings drew him closer to spirituality. Conrado del Carril, before dying, had loaned him *The Great Initiates* by Édouard Schuré. Later he had read books on the occult and Eastern religions, especially Buddhism, areas that began to obsess him during the trip to India with Adán Diehl. In March 1927, Adelina and Ricardo left with Delia and the González Garaño couple, embarking on the *Massilia*, the same boat that had brought them to Argentina after Delia separated. Shortly after arriving in Paris, Ricardo's health took a turn for the worse. Looking for tranquility, for an escape from the Parisian summer just beginning, Adelina, Ricardo and Delia went to Arcachon, a spa near Burdeos. There Güiraldes continued his work on *El Sendero* [The Path], more a spiritual book than a literary one, inspired by *The Great Initiates*, Patanjali's aphorisms and the Gospel of Sri Rama Krishna. It was a pilgrimage in which he assimilated Brahmanical wisdom and Christian principles. Delia and Adelina delved into the mysterious aspects of this spirituality with him, repeating Ricardo's favorite expression: "We grow weary of everything but knowing."

But the writer's health grew worse. In Bordeaux they had to hire an ambulance carriage to bring them back to Paris. The González Garaño couple lent them their apartment at 7 Rue Edmond Valentin, and Justa del Carril arrived in Paris to help her sisters. Delia and Justa were Ricardo's nurses, since Adelina was in denial that her husband was going to die.

The illness grew painful. He was given morphine injections. He suffered from hemorrhages that sent him into bouts of tremendous anguish. But the writer's last days were full of tranquility, an effect of his own contemplative thoughts and the morphine. The news that he had won the National Literature Prize, for *Don Segundo Sombra*, arrived just few days before his death, when he was unable to appreciate the recognition.

"So it is, or so it will be." These are the last words of his that Delia managed to hear. Spoken with a smile, a moment before dying, in the afternoon of October 8, 1926.

At the church of Saint-Pierre de Gros Caillou, at 92 Rue St. Dominique, a few blocks away from the apartment of the González Garaño couple, a solemn mass took place. It was attended by French friends like Adrienne Monnier, other writers and many Argentines who were in Paris.

The body of Ricardo Güiraldes was embalmed and sent home on the steamboat *Avila*. It was a sad trip for Delia and Adelina. They arrived in Buenos Aires on November 15, where the family was waiting for them, along with friends from *Proa* and *Martín*

Fierro, and the President of the Republic, Marcelo T. de Alvear. From there they moved to Retiro Station, and then departed in numerous carriages toward San Antonio de Areco, where Ricardo was buried.

Adelina went to the countryside to gather and arrange the papers her husband had left behind. Delia stayed with her.

CHAPTER 4

1929–1930

B ack at her apartment on Paraguay Street, Delia rejoined the intellectual life of Buenos Aires. She took up painting classes again, this time with Juan del Prete, a thirty-year-old son of Italian immigrants who had been raised in the neighborhood of La Boca. He still wasn't the recognized painter that he would become, but he had already discovered his unique technique of using not a paintbrush but a spatula, which gave his vibrant landscapes new depths of material and density. These studies from nature offered Delia an escape from academic drawing, which wasn't her forte. With the spatula she felt artistically free for the first time. But just as before, no one thought her paintings deserved any particular attention.

Her friends preferred her conversations, her witticisms and her imitations of them during the Thursday lunches she organized. Paellas were provided by Josefa, the Andalucian maid who took care of the house and arranged everything for impractical

Delia. Those lunches brought together the many foreign artists passing through Buenos Aires, and they usually ended with splendid concerts by Ricardo Viñes, the Spanish pianist who had taught Poulenc and was a painstaking collector of contemporary music. Delia was strict, observing the behaviors and manners of her guests, and deciding whom to include and exclude. Antón Giulio Bragaglia, the founder of the Experimental Theater of Rome, arrived to give a series of talks for the Amigos del Arte. At the Copper Kettle on Florida Street, Delia jokingly pointed out to him that he bit his nails, to which the Italian replied: "Yes, and also the nails on my lovers' toes." Never again did he appear on her guest list.

It was during these years that Delia met María Rosa Oliver, who would become one of her lifelong female friends. María Rosa coped with the disability of childhood paralysis by applying her intense intelligence to the Amigos del Arte. She and Luis Saslavsky organized an experimental theater for the society, where new generations of children from conservative families started to meet and form friendships, following the trail that had been blazed by Victoria, Delia, Ricardo and their friends.

In 1929 Delia left again for Paris. She wasn't enjoying life in Buenos Aires. She had stayed for two years to be closer to her family after so many deaths and misfortunes, and yet, despite being settled at the epicenter of the city, she felt a desire to explore other paths, other possibilities that couldn't be glimpsed from where she was. Bound by tight ties, she felt she was stagnating.

Through the Martín Fierro group, she had met famous people like Saint-Exupéry and Marinetti, but they were fleeting interactions, and she merely fulfilled the role of an aristocratic woman with intellectual leanings. True, she was liberated, but her belonging was contingent upon her social privilege, and this left her with the same feeling of emptiness as the social successes of her youth. She wanted to escape this condition. At forty-six years old, she didn't want to continue her restless wandering.

Paris had always given her a sensation of freedom. And there was no specter of Adán Diehl haunting the city. The previous year he had finally convinced the Costa family to cede him the lands in Formentor. Tito Citaddini, who lived in Pollença and directed a painting school there, convinced Diehl to set up a hotel on the new property. Through the influence of his mother at the Torcquist Bank in Buenos Aires, he acquired the millions that were necessary to begin construction. Only a madman like Adán could have plunged himself into such a gigantic undertaking. Out of nowhere there came electric lighting, telephones, drinkable water, a road to the hotel, gardens and a magnificent golf course, in addition to an enormous and lavish house. In June 1929, the Hotel Formentor was inaugurated with a spectacular party attended by numerous celebrities from Europe. Diehl also got married again, this time to María Elena Rafaela Popolizio.

In Paris, Delia rented an apartment at 44 Rue Elysée Reclus, a street near the Eiffel tower where her mother also had an apartment at number 17. There she settled in with Josefa, whose indispensable company was evident in her perfect reply to Delia's question about a Cubist painting by Picasso.

"What do you think of it, Josefa?"

"Madame, it's like he painted nothin'."

Prepared at last to take her painting seriously, Delia learned through friends that Fernand Léger, one of the pillars of the Paris school, had just opened L'Academie Moderne in his studio at 86 Rue Notre Dame de Champs. She went to study with him.

A simple and solitary man, Léger had very precise ideas about the world, and his art was based on his way of seeing. At first he was violently criticized for including mechanical elements and industrial processes in his work, but soon he consolidated a mode of expression all his own. Yet he had furious detractors like Matisse, and was never recognized by the official art world. His obsession with machines was a reflection of his interest in people within their workplace. Neither paintings nor art were worthwhile to him unless their aesthetic was at the disposal of the everyday. Léger wanted to change the gloomy atmosphere of the factories and hospitals, and these ideas led him to collaborate with Le Corbusier on architectural projects, where their innovations were welcomed.

Léger's ideas had their origin in his desire for liberty and justice. He was against economic disparities and the exploitation of the working class. Inspired by the historical materialism of Marx, he belonged to the French Communist Party. Léger's intelligence, his humanism, and his ideas about painting were rejuvenating for Delia, who felt anxious for change.

Delia's admiration for Léger briefly led to a more intimate relationship, of which we do not have concrete details, only rumors instisting that this friendship, which lasted until the painter's death, had a romantic aspect.

With Léger, Delia gained access to a new side of Paris. Despite her many years spent in the city, she was still a foreigner from Latin America. What she knew about the avant-garde and modernity came from newspapers, museum visits, ballet performances, social gatherings and a few passing contacts at Adrienne Monnier's bookshop. She didn't have access to the private lives of these personalities.

Now, from a place of intimacy, Delia met a wider circle of artists and writers, among them Pablo Picasso, Blaise Cendrars, Le Corbusier, Louis Aragon and Paul Éluard.

Delia, 1940.

Stalin had just expelled Leon Trotsky from the Soviet Union, and many voices objected to this treatment of one of the heroes of the October Revolution. Art was no longer enough; artists were expected to show political commitment. The upheaval in the world was too serious for intellectuals to remain indifferent to the dangers to freedom and thought posed by the fascist dictatorship of Mussolini in Italy and the advance of the Nazis in Germany. The Soviet Union and the Communist Party developed strategies to convince intellectuals of the necessity of a commitment to peace and liberty. The movement began in France, among artists who adhered to the aesthetic values of the Soviet revolution. Even the surrealists, who in their manifestos and attitudes were diametrically opposed to any system, enrolled in the party. Conspicuous nihilists like Aragon, Breton, Éluard and Péret joined its ranks, even if nearly all of them would in time be expelled from the party for their deviations. Louis Aragon emerged at world congresses as a brilliant figure who would bring together the artists of the West.

These ideas of equality and justice produced a strong transformation in Delia. Everything she heard and saw, all the conversations and dilemmas, revealed to her a vision of another reality, one that was boundless and all-encompassing. Only now did she understand her dissatisfaction and the restlessness that she had been feeling for so many years. They derived precisely from the lack of a higher commitment, something she hadn't yet found on her life journey.

Delia spoke her views openly. Used to giving an opinion, she knew very well how to forge herself a place. She spoke slowly, never raising her voice and yet making herself heard, as for instance when Le Corbusier, invited by Amigos del Arte to give a few talks in Buenos Aires, asked whether it would be worth losing two months to travel to a faraway country. Delia, irritated, explained to him what her country was like and how absurd his contempt was, and convinced him to make the trip. When he came back from Buenos Aires, he said he had benefited from the experience and thanked her for her insistence.

But it was hard to separate herself from her social sphere, and once again it drew her back in. Victoria Ocampo arrived in Paris. Her father had died and she had decided to begin serious work on a new project: a Latin American magazine that recruited its authors from the United States and Europe. The idea was to create a bridge for exchange between two worlds that were ignorant of each other. She had come to make contacts, and to sign up writers who interested her. Before dying, her father had told her that a cultural project would only lead to her ruin. She thought he might be right, but the idea of the magazine consolidated her scattered literary doubts and intimate ambitions too well. She asked Delia to accompany her on these trips.

But first, Victoria had to fulfill a commitment to Rabindranath Tagore, with whom she shared a long friendship. She had promised to visit him in the south of France, to see his paintings and drawings.

The two friends left by car in the company of the driver and Victoria's faithful maid Fani, heading toward Cap Martin near Montecarlo where Tagore lived. Fani had a bad habit of talking nonstop, which exasperated the travelers. Victoria ate nougat throughout the nine-hour journey, and began to feel ill. Delia forced the driver to stop at Avignon for lunch. At last they arrived at Villa Dumure, the home of the Jewish philanthropist Alberto Khan, where Tagore was working.

Thanks to Victoria's contacts and money, Tagore's images, which she saw as curious decorative works, debuted in Paris on May 2, 1930 at the Galerie Pigalle.

A few days later, Delia and Victoria set out for New York. It was a decisive trip for Victoria's project, as she planned to meet there with Waldo Frank, one of the most enthusiastic supporters of the magazine. Frank was convinced that all of America should be united and that intellectuals and artists were responsible for creating a common base for thought rooted in the unique identities of each people.

The travelers settled into the Sherry Netherland Hotel, located on Fifth Avenue and 59th Street, facing Central Park. At seven dollars a night, it was one of the finest hotels in the area.

Despite the economic crisis, financial disasters, and the bankruptcies of banks and industries that had erupted the previous year in the New York Stock Exchange, the city was a much different spectacle from the one that Delia had observed ten years before, during her honeymoon with Adán. Incredible skyscrapers had shot up and New York had taken on a cosmopolitan air, as its population increased by several million.

Waldo Frank introduced them to various people, in a tight schedule of outings and meals. There were visits to Harlem where the sound of church spirituals impressed them, and to the Cotton Club in Broadway to hear Duke Ellington play. There were also meetings with the Soviet filmmaker Sergei Eisenstein, whom Delia had met in Paris, and who had accepted a contract with Paramount Pictures to avoid the political tensions in his home country.

The two friends enjoyed their trip despite very having different personalities. Delia tended to triumph through her lightness and charm. More festive than serious, and easily distracted, she had a special ease for entering into quick sympathy with anybody. Meanwhile Victoria had a more imposing beauty and was more cautious, more reasonable, more shy and more conscious of her importance, never anxious to please. The two women understood one another wonderfully well, said Victoria, because it was hard not to get along with Delia.

Victoria talked with Waldo Frank about her project, about the writers in Europe who had promised to contribute. The magazine was taking shape.

Delia, despite her apparent superficiality, lived in a permanent duality of lightness and depth. She talked with Frank about the one topic Victoria avoided: politics. Frank's communist sympathies were well known, and thanks to her new friends in Paris, Delia was also very interested.

After a month, they returned by boat to Buenos Aires. During the long journey through the Panama Canal, disembarking at every port where the boat docked, they arrived one day in a dusty and solitary town. Walking through the streets, Delia suddenly noticed an enormous white hanging flower. She pointed it out to Victoria: "Have you ever seen such beauty in your life?" Victoria laughed. "Obviously I've seen it, and you have too, it's an Angel's Trumpet!" It was a common flower in South America. In her distraction, Delia had a flair for discovering something new in what she'd seen before.

Victoria would launch the magazine *Sur* the following year.

Delia's fate remained uncertain.

CHAPTER 5

1931–1933

The financial situation of the del Carril family went from bad to worse. The estate's administrators were far from shrewd. They believed that the world's crises were only temporary, and that everything would be resolved in the long run. They never suspected that the hereditary fortune might collapse.

Delia wasn't a big spender. She didn't afford herself great luxuries. She wasn't interested in jewels or expensive dresses. For her, the income from the building she had inherited was enough. With the sale of a few properties in Mar del Plata, she bought a plot of land called "Cerro Blanco" in the Jachal region, in the northern part of San Juan province. Everybody told her it wasn't good for anything, but she continued to believe the lands were a safe investment. The problem was that her money didn't reach her regularly when she was living abroad. She took advantage of her stay in Buenos Aires to look for new administrators, ones who were committed to her needs.

She decided to go back to Paris when General Uriburu's military coup began to brew in Buenos Aires. Spurred on by civilians with fascist ideas, Uriburu deprived the constitutional president and Radical Party member Hipólito Yrigoyen of his position in September 1930. It was the first coup in the history of the Republic.

In Paris, Delia's friendship with Louis Aragon and his wife Elsa Triolet became more intimate. Fernand Léger had left for the United States. Once again, in an almost reflexive act, Delia took up painting classes, enrolling in an open studio at 2 Rue Jules Chaplain, led by André Lothe.

During the '20s André Lothe had been active along with Georges Braque and Juan Gris in the movement of synthetic cubism. He was a critic and a scholar of painting, with a book about landscape that is still required reading for art students.

He was Delia's maestro at the Grande Chaumière, which consisted of a big studio with seats in a circle for artists, with a model in the center who changed poses throughout the day. Delia continued to struggle with drawing, but her special intensity was always recognized. Her drawings had something different about them, a masculine strength. Long before, when she had painted with Güiraldes, those who had seen both their paintings confused Delia's with Ricardo's, which featured a much gentler style.

Aragon had come back from the Soviet Union, a trip that influenced him so much he committed decisively to the communist ideology, and in doing so finally abandoned his old companions, the surrealists.

Delia internalized Marxism little by little, reading everything that she could find. She read *Capital* quickly, with the same ease that one reads a novel. She read *The Class Struggles in France* with the same interest. The utopia of communism, its long-term vision of a society in which everyone receives and contributes according to his or her needs and abilities, filled her with a fervent enthusiasm. She found answers to her own contradictions, and felt that she'd discovered her calling. It seemed to her that everything she'd experienced was resolved in this ideology, which satisfied some of her emptiness. The great obstacles of confused bourgeois life were all written in its pages. Here was what she'd been looking for.

Like a good convert, communism became her only topic of conversation. She knew the *Communist Manifesto* of 1848 almost by heart, and read any book about it that fell into her hands. She felt she'd spent too much time ignorant of politics, and considered it her obligation to bring herself up-to-date.

Her conviction was strengthened by the people who surrounded her. Communist organizations were spreading throughout Europe. A letter arrived from Argentina written by María Rosa Oliver, the friend she'd recently made at Amigos del Arte, who to her surprise confided that she had read the same books and also felt that illuminating enthusiasm.

In her book *La vida cotidiana* [Everyday Life], María Rosa Oliver would write, "The *Communist Manifesto* dazzled me more than anything else I have ever read; however, even though I felt that Marxist economic theory adheres to reality like a tree firmly rooted in the soil, the philosophy of historical materialism seemed to float in the air, as much at the mercy of different winds as any of the other philosophies with which I've tried to identify myself in vain. But the atheism didn't shock me—what could have shocked me!—the individual and collective behavior of those who proclaim themselves believers in God has exhausted my capacity for scandal. In contrast, I saw in Marxism—and for the moment I continue to see—the only valid means to carry into practice the phrase 'Love thy neighbor as thyself.'"

Delia and Pablo at Isla Negra, 1942.

At last Delia joined the French Communist Party, registering herself as a painter in the newly created Association of Revolutionary Writers and Artists, after having been convinced by Louis Aragon that she could strengthen the relationship between communist intellectuals and non-communists.

Although this act did not represent any great change to her daily activities with sympathizers and members of the party, in her private life it provided a vitally important foundation. She had committed herself to others. She felt useful. The uneasiness of her past, the wandering and searching, came to an end. Once and for all, she had severed ties with her uncomfortable double life, caught between her privilege on the one hand and her intense personal experiences on the other.

Delia's decision, which she announced in euphoric letters to her friends in Argentina, was totally rejected by her family. They simply couldn't believe it. This was a real scandal, more so than any of her past eccentricities. A profound change had taken place in the upper bourgeoisie. Families with a certain liberalism used to have been able to forgive private faults, if the trouble remained under wraps. But that was before. The popular class was beginning to speak out. The upper classes decided to close ranks. Thorough strictness now prevailed, and there was no longer any understanding for those who failed to comply. A political turn like Delia's was the very worst possible transgression.

CHAPTER 6

1934–1936

All at once, in a series of coincidences, a merging of several different paths, the idea of going to Spain appeared. A letter from Tota Atucha, Delia's lifelong friend who had married a Spanish count, proposed a meeting in Madrid. Rafael Alberti and María Teresa León, passing through Paris from Moscow on their way to Madrid, met Delia at Victoria Ocampo's house. Through outings and conversations, they convinced her that her income would go much further in Spain. They insisted that everything important was happening there.

Spain was living through the Republican Era. Everybody watched with astonishment what was happening in Mussolini's Italy. In Germany, Hitler had risen to the top as Chancellor of the Hindenburg government, and the power of the Nazi party was uncontrollable. In Portugal, António de Oliveira Salazar had just established a dictatorship. Spain became the face of the coin on which the entire forward-thinking world was betting.

Delia was about to turn fifty years old, but she still looked young, ambitious, and full of energy. "When I want to describe beauty and grace, the image of Delia comes to mind," wrote María Teresa León in her *Memorias de la melancolía* [Memoirs of Melancholy].

Overnight she left her apartment in Paris and once again filled her Innovation brand trunk with whatever she could fit into its drawers. The rest that had been accumulated, everything in excess, could be left behind. Of course it was Josefa who had to worry about everything, as Delia always had difficulty organizing and tended to lose things. In the middle of winter, at the end of January 1934, they took the train to Madrid.

The city came as a complete surprise. The image of childhood that she had kept with her was limited to the Sacred Heart school, strolls through the parks that she remembered as silent and empty, royal ceremonies, and a short-lived family friendship with the now-exiled Alfonso XIII. She couldn't believe what she saw this time. People filled the streets in a permanent movement that amazed her. Everybody was helping each other out. The Alberti couple opened the doors of their friendships wide open.

The political situation in Spain was less promising than she'd hoped.

The Second Republic had its origin in the right-wing dictatorship of Miguel Primo de Rivera, begun in 1923 with the support of the army, the Catholic church, the political right and the king. Student and worker protests—products of the world economic crisis of 1929—accelerated its end. Primo de Rivera resigned in January 1930. The monarchy, weakened by its support of the dictatorship, attempted to restore normalcy with a constitutional government. But a great coalition of leftist opposition produced the Republican electoral triumph of April 1931, which

Image courtesy Pablo Neruda Foundation

Llamas, engraving made in 1954.

forced the king to abdicate and go into exile, to first in France and then in Italy.

Once the Republic had been proclaimed, a decisive period of change ushered in new social and economic bases that promoted the modernization of the country. A new mentality was felt in all spheres. Agrarian and educational reforms increased the social agitation that the anarchists had provoked. Aligning itself with the conservatives, the Catholic church closed its ranks against civil matrimony and state education, which had created thousands of schools to combat the illiteracy that affected forty percent of the population. In addition, a Falangist Party with a fascist strain was founded, led by José Antonio Primo de Rivera, the son of the previous dictator. Catholic conservatives and Falangists won the elections at the Courts in November 1933. Left and right, secularists and Catholics entered into battle at that moment, radicalizing the conflicting factions.

These were the circumstances at the moment Delia arrived in Madrid. But reality and daily life always weave in additional complexities, fine threads that move within individual experience, and leave such broad strokes for history alone.

The powerful cultural movement taking place in the Republic relied on the international solidarity of intellectuals and artists, who came to Spain to live the experience of a people in turmoil.

Delia settled into an apartment on Goya Street, and immediately began to make contacts and immerse herself in the events.

She approached the Alliance of Intellectuals, the operating base of the Communist Party where Alberti was secretary and María Teresa León had a prominent place. She also registered at the San Fernando Academy to continue her ever-interrupted painting courses. Soon afterward she joined the Workers' Choir, where her voice quickly made an impression on the others.

Within two months, she felt she had the lay of the land. Due to her knowledge of English and French, Delia was one of those responsible for accompanying and serving as a translator to the foreigners who arrived every day to join the Republicans. She also translated documents from all over the world at the crowded office of the Alliance.

This change in her life was greater than anything she had imagined. Madrid, the Spanish, the excitement of her obligations, the usefulness of so many hours busy at jobs with such precise and necessary ends—all this seemed to be made for the vitality and energy of her character. The days grew short with the back-and-forth of important conversations, as different people came together to create a mystical strength capable of rising up to overcome any obstacle. The constant discussion of current events could alternately strengthen or weaken the positions of the various factions struggling for power. This stimulated Delia to read the newspapers with a dedication that steadily increased her political convictions, and helped her discover the passion and certainty of her longings.

The effervescence of those days was due, in part, to those powerfully human meetings, to the heated and exhilarating conversations of the groups that filled the city's wine bars and taverns where old friends met and new ones were added, where loves were born and there was always something to celebrate.

One of the few private and privileged spaces in those years, where monarchists and Catholics still co-existed with furious atheists, poets, bullfighters, artists, politicians and countesses, was the house of the Minister Counselor at the Chilean Embassy, Carlos Morla Lynch, and his wife, Bebé Vicuña, on Velázquez Street facing the Hotel Wellington.

Carlos Morla was a conservative Catholic diplomat who adored noble titles, but he had a sensitive weakness for artists. He himself composed music for poems by young poets, and although he hated it when anyone sang "The Internationale", which in those days was quite a common event, he could forgive this in exchange for the poetic quality and personality of a rare talent.

Delia, just after her arrival, was invited to one of those social gatherings by Tota Atucha, who despite her liberal ideas was married to the Count of Cuevas de Vera. Rafael Alberti and María Teresa were also in the group, along with an infinite number of poets. It was there that Delia first heard the name of Federico García Lorca, Morla's closest friend, who in those days was enjoying a resounding theatrical success in Buenos Aires. She also met Luis Enrique Délano and his wife Lola Falcón, just arrived from Chile, with whom she immediately became friends.

The social gatherings at the Morla house were lively and entertaining. Perhaps out of respect for the owner of the house, politics was sidestepped in conversation. Instead, people talked about theatrical premieres, new books, poetry, and everything else that enhanced the attraction of a refined get-together.

For Delia, all of this, her politically engaged work and her meetings with people who were so interesting and different from what she had known, meant complete happiness. She went almost every afternoon to Correos Brewery, where the poets met, and where every table presented an opportunity to talk until late at night. She had a fantastic ability to remain fresh, although she slept very little. The excitement of her new life was too great, and she wasn't going to waste it sleeping. There were always obligations, urgent matters, but she didn't miss these café gatherings.

In the middle of April, like a whirlwind, García Lorca returned from Argentina. He was happy, radiant, overflowing with money as never before. His play *Bodas de sangre* [Blood Wedding], in the interpretation of Lola Membrives, had been so successful that the last performance was transmitted by radio throughout all of Argentina. This was followed by his presentation of *La zapatera prodigiosa* [The Shoemaker's Prosperous Wife], another triumph, and *Mariana Pineda*. Federico, considering this last to be a weaker work, was afraid it would dull his reputation, but just the opposite happened. He returned to Spain with not only recognition but economic independence from his parents. He came dressed very elegantly, in white linen suits that had never been seen before in Spain. In his honor, a great party was given at the Florida Hotel, where the poet staged a show that left everybody astonished. A puppet theater performed *El retablillo de don Cristóbal* [The Puppet Play of Don Cristóbal], which he had written, with an interlude that adapted a play by Cervantes. The celebration continued afterward with a meal at the house of the poet Pedro Salinas.

Delia had met Federico days before at the house of Carlos Morla, and they'd crossed paths several evenings at the Correos Brewery. The writer's conversation had delighted her, and he'd been fascinated by her elegance and insolence, a certain ironic tone in her way of speaking that seemed to him to be a typically Argentine trait, recently discovered on his trip. The poet admired Argentine women, as he considered them to be more liberated. As he put it: Argentine women are immediately great friends. They talked about Buenos Aires, and she asked García Lorca about all the friends of hers he'd visited.

Always nudging the people who interested him toward the theater, Federico suggested that she participate in a group that he had helped set up, run by Pura Ucelay. It was the theater group of the Feminine Culture Club, known as the Anfistora Theater, a name that evoked ancient Greece but was just one of the many words that the poet had invented. Look at her, here she is… the Anfistora of Granada, he had once said about an old maid at his father's house. And he'd gone about creating an anfistora type, a full-figured, fat, blonde and very smartly-dressed woman. Perhaps the director of the group didn't know the burlesque origin of the word, but the group flaunted the name with great pride. Federico gave them some of his works and directed the staging. So Delia found herself helping with the selection of the wardrobe for *Liliom* by Ferenc Molnár, which debuted with notable success when it was directed by Federico at the Teatro Español.

At Carlos Morla's social gatherings that May, there was talk about the imminent arrival of the Chilean poet Pablo Neruda. Federico had met him in Buenos Aires, and the two had struck up a friendship based on mutual admiration. Delia had read some poems from the book *Residencia en la tierra* [Residence on Earth], which had appeared in the magazine *Proa* in Buenos Aires, but she didn't have any further information. "Do you know this Neruda?" she asked Lola Falcón.

Who was the Neruda that arrived in Madrid on June 1, 1934?

"Pale, an ashen paleness, large and narrow eyes like almonds of black glass, he laughs at every opportunity but without joy, passively. His hair is also very black and poorly combed, and his hands are gray. No elegance whatsoever. His pockets are full of jotted notes and newspapers. What captivates me in him is his voice: a slow, monotonous, nostalgic voice, as if tired, but suggestive and full of charm." Carlos Morla wrote this in his diary the day of the poet's arrival, and it seems to be such an accurate description that many continue to use it.

Neruda was about to turn thirty years old, and he'd been appointed consul in Barcelona. His life hadn't been easy. Born in Parral, a town in the south of Chile, his mother had died within a month of his birth. He was raised further to the south, in Temuco, where his father was a railway worker. Educated at a public high school, he hated mathematics and loved books. He wrote poems. When he was very young he moved to Santiago, and began studies to be a French teacher at the University of Chile, but writing was his main interest. He published his first work, *Crepuscu-lario* [Book of Twilight], when he was nineteen years old. His father didn't understand this passion, and didn't accept his poet son. Neruda participated in a bohemia of bars and poverty. He began to feel anguish in Chile. In 1924 he edited *Veinte poemas de amor y una canción desesperada* [Twenty Love Poems and a Song of Despair]. The applause was resounding but he made enemies along the way. Nobody accepted him or recognized his greatness, which had come out of nowhere. He kept working and wrote new books: *Tentativa del hombre infinito* [Venture of the Infinite Man], *El habitante y su esperanza* [The Inhabitant and His Hope], *Anillos* [Rings] in collaboration with his friend Tomás Lago, and *El hondero entusiasta* [The Enthusiastic Slingsman]. Some were published, while others waited: poetry doesn't sell.

Having secured an appointment that allowed him to leave the Chile that suffocated him, he went as consul to Ceylon, Java and Singapore. The loneliness and the feeling of abandonment the East produced in him gave rise to a new and extraordinary volume of poetry: *Residence on Earth*. In Java he married a Dutch woman, María Antonieta Hagenaar Vogelzang. He returned to Chile, where one hundred copies of *Residence on Earth* were published, as well as another edition of *Twenty Poems*. He brought his Dutch wife with him, but she wasn't well-liked by his friends. Feeling restless, Neruda moved to Buenos Aires in 1933 after being named consul there, and then to Barcelona.

When he arrived in Madrid, he lodged at the Mediodía Hotel in the popular neighborhood of Atocha. Federico and some friends had gone to wait for him at the station. From there they went to the Baviera Bar on Alcalá Street, where they met with Carlos Morla, who took them to lunch at his house. The next morning Neruda showed up at the diplomat's house. He was very pale and felt nauseous, thanks to the intense partying of the previous night. The host offered him a bed, and Neruda got some rest. After a while Gabriela Mistral came to see him. She was now consul in Madrid, but she had met Pablo when he was very young, in the south of Chile. Gabriela had always been interested in his work, so different from her own. Futurist poet, she said. She dedicated herself to reading his verses while the poet was asleep.

At night, the Morla house filled with people who had come to meet him. The party and its details are recorded in his diary: Federico did a dance with a rug wrapped around him, and Bebé Vicuña sang compositions by Carlos on the guitar. Her lyrics were the poems of Alberti, Cernuda, Altolaguirre, Ramón Jiménez and of course García Lorca. Very late at night, when a certain calm descended, Neruda read some of the poems from *Residence on Earth*. The poet's voice boomed out from the middle of the living room. "We found ourselves captivated by a force of great proportions," Morla would later comment.

To lighten the atmosphere, after the reading of this heavy prose, Federico recited some of his *Poemas del cante jondo* [Poems of the Deep Song], and then Acario Cotapos, the Chilean musician, finished off the night with one of his masterful acts of imitation.

Cotapos was a short and chubby man, maniacal and totally eccentric. He was scared to death of germs and infections, and he fled in terror from thin people, seeing them as victims of tuberculosis who might pass on their disease to him. He didn't give his hand to anybody, or, if he had no choice, he cleaned himself meticulously afterward with a handkerchief. He turned on lights and opened doors with his shirt cuff, making sure that his hands didn't touch any handles, switches or knobs. At the movie theater he changed places if he suspected illness in his neighbors. He always found some detail that pointed to a danger in the person who approached him. Nobody appreciated his music, but he had a gift for imitation, and an imagination for inventing situations and characters that made him an obligatory guest at any gathering. During his recent stay in Paris, it was known that when he found himself short of money, he had entertained the owners of a Russian restaurant and eaten without paying for many days, parodying sessions of the Soviet Parliament and immersing himself in the most absurd problems, finding it incredibly easy to reproduce the onomatopoeia of highly complicated languages that nobody else knew. Wars, changes of the guard, advances of cavalry and the presentation of credentials were the much-requested acts that made everybody split their sides in laughter.

There are several versions of the story about how Delia and Pablo Neruda met. The most likely one takes place on the night of that party at Carlos Morla's house.

The poet stayed for only a few days in Madrid, and then went back to his job in Barcelona. The Consul General of Chile Tulio Maqueira, his direct superior, quickly understood that Neruda wasn't a man for numbers and offices, and that bureaucracy was not his strength. He told him to return to Madrid, that the people who suited him were there. In August, Neruda made the definitive move to Madrid, accompanied by his wife, who was pregnant.

Rafael Alberti claims that Delia and Pablo met at his apartment on Marqués de Urquijo Street, when Neruda presented himself there with María Antonieta Hagenaar.

Delia's own memory is that she saw him for the first time one night at the Correos Brewery, when he sat next to her, "put his arm around my shoulder, and that's how we stayed".

Could there have been two people any more different? It's difficult and risky to explain the origins of an interest, the unthinkable reasons that bring a couple together and make love possible. The mystery of why him, and why her, can lead to a number of questions without answer, in which there is surely more absurdity than logic. In this case, however, there were motives that time would make comprehensible, even if at the start there was only a powerful intuition, in the guise of attraction.

They more or less fit the archetypes of the eternal romantic stories. Looking at them face to face, both seemed to be perfect complements of what was lacking in the other. She had a past, almost majestic in its history, and an ample dose of beauty, originality, intelligence, charm and worldliness to lavish on others. He was much younger, with a melancholy, sad, anxious personality, as well as a literary gift, a great poet but mostly unrecognized.

The reality of this idyllic picture is that few people knew that their meeting had been romantic, and saw it as nothing more than an intellectual friendship. María Teresa León thought that she noticed something in their way of looking at each another when Pablo and Delia arrived at her house very early one morning for breakfast, sleepless after having done the rounds at bars and taverns all night with friends.

Neruda's private life was complicated. His marriage to Maruca had been the consequence of an unbearable solitude during his time in the East. She was an increasingly silent and absent woman, distant from the life of the poet and his friends, and the exciting bohemia of Madrid at that time. There was also his situation as a poet. Even if he was recognized as a dazzling voice in private circles, he was having a hard time getting published. The acceptance that he'd received was a long way from real success and security. Uncertainty weighed on him.

His life in Madrid seemed to begin with promising signs. The Alberti couple found an apartment for him in the Argüelles neighborhood on Hilarión Eslava Street, in the Casa de las Flores, very near the university campus that had just been built. Pablo and María Antonieta Hagenaar settled in.

Their apartment turned into a meeting place for poets and artists, all of whom arrived at the start of the evening. The most regular were Federico, Manuel Altolaguirre (a printer and poet), his wife Concha Méndez, José Caballero (a painter, set designer and great collaborator with García Lorca on the legendary traveling theater of La Barraca), Acario Cotapos naturally, Santiago Ontañón (a set designer and journalistic correspondent, assistant to María Teresa León at the Theater of Art and Propaganda of the Alliance of Intellectuals), José Bergamín (a poet, editor of the magazine *Cruz y Raya*) and the painter Maruja Mallo. When they arrived, anything might happen, from poetry readings to the tireless acts of Acario, who in those days made an impression with his brilliant performance of the burial of the recently deceased German president, Paul Hindenburg, including speeches by Hitler and Goering and all the bells and whistles of parades and volleys of gunfire, to which García Lorca collaborated with his flair. Wine was drunk, lots of wine, along with the Chinchón anisette that had become Neruda's favorite. If it weren't the burial of Hindenburg, it might be the adventures of the Horned Boar, another character from the Cotapos mythology, based on a neighbor of his who snored so loudly that the walls shook every night, or the confession of a naïve peasant girl, interpreted by Federico with a handkerchief tied around his head, in front of a chastising old-fashioned priest, Acario, in an act that could easily last for an hour with the description of the most incredible temptations and falls of the peasant girl and the carrying out of highly unusual penances. After this, the group headed outside to other ceremonies that they deemed essential, such as the inauguration of nonexistent statues, or the delivery of stirring but cheeky speeches before historical monuments. The night always ended with the light of dawn.

In the midst of the uproar it was hard for Delia to find a moment to talk about serious things, political events, the actions undertaken by the Alliance of Intellectuals, the support for foreigners who continued to arrive in Madrid, or the reasons it was imperative to increase aid to this or that project. She took every opportunity to involve people in collaborating on these topics. Her life had undergone a complete transformation, and this transformation needed an external sign. Her friends gave her a new name: the Ant.

Federico had asked Delia to do something to avoid the departure of Acario Cotapos from Madrid, as his grant was ending and he didn't have the money to stay there. He was planning to return to Chile, and this could not be permitted. Delia took it as an assignment and started to gather funds from friends, insisting, moving from one place to another, with the diligence and vigor she put into everything. "Look, you have to help," was her repeated phrase. When Isaías Cabezón, the Chilean painter, saw all this energy in action, he said: "This Delia is an ant." The new name was quickly adopted by everyone.

The young Spanish poets, led by Federico, were growing in importance. Neruda's arrival was a decisive contribution to a new form of modern poetry that broke with traditional images, incorporating new elements that hadn't previously been considered poetic material. Along the way they met with the most heated detractors, among them the renowned writer Juan Ramón Jiménez.

The author of *Platero y yo* [Platero and I] felt himself to be something like the judge of what was or wasn't poetry, and he delivered his decisions in exaggerated verdicts. He stopped greeting José Ortega y Gasset for a long time because he kept a small bust of Beethoven on the piano in his home, an unbearable offense to elegance. He gave up greeting Pérez de Ayala when he discovered that hams hung in the larder of his house, which Juan Ramón considered to be terrible poetic judgment. He used sarcasm to refer to publications he didn't like. He called *Revista de Occidente* "Disorient," and *Cruz y Raya* run by José Bergamín, which published many of the poets who ignored his advice, "Mediocre Mag." In his own home he displayed outlandish attitudes. During the social gatherings organized by his wife Zenobia Camprubí, to avoid greeting the guests, he would cross through the hall covered by a folding screen, so that only his feet could be seen. Neruda's arrival upset him, and he began to launch furious attacks against the new poetry in his Sunday articles for the newspaper *El Sol.* The young people, without responding to his criticisms, got even by phoning him up pretending to be the donkey Platero, certain of the rage that this would provoke in Juan Ramón.

The group of friends was also useful for maintaining the appearance of a strictly intellectual relationship between Delia and Pablo. Due to her personality and her advanced state of pregnancy, Maruca Hagenaar was mentally distant from what was happening outside her home, but Neruda was still attached to his established life and was afraid of her reactions. It suited him to indulge in a new stimulation that didn't demand drastic changes. In the poet's character there was a strong need for security and shelter, and for the moment, Maruca fulfilled this role. "We can't all be be mothers," the writer María Luisa Bombal commented, referring to this trait of Neruda's. Delia's enthusiasm thus unfolded in the spaces that Maruca did not occupy, in the many places where she was second to none.

It's possible that Neruda initially resisted this woman of the world, a world that was unknown to him, wary perhaps of being the object of a whim by an older aristocratic woman who in many aspects overwhelmed him, and who seemed to know all the secrets of social grace—a refined woman who could also seem distant, who dominated situations with an innate ease, and who had the precise words for everyone, one who imposed respect and was concrete in her proposals, yet at the same time scattered, distracted, unpredictable.

Every afternoon at the Correos Brewery, the program for the night was decided. From there they left for the theater, the cinema or a social gathering at the house of Carlos Morla, if there was a special reading or a well-known person. Or they might eat at the Granja del Enar on Alcalá Street, or simply go out walking down the streets with a bottle of Chinchón, stopping at the stalls in the plazas to eat a few calamari fried in thick olive oil, tucked into a sugared bread roll. They would stay talking for hours, since the idea was to stretch out the night that often ended at Pablo's house, with both well-known and new friends, who themselves invited further acquaintances. Sometimes the men would say good night and continue on to Satán, a nightclub at 60 Atocha Street managed by the young Cuban Mario Carreño, who acted as artistic and social director of the "Infernal Parties" at which Monserra champagne, La Guita manzanilla sherry and Sarracina cider flowed. The Lecuona Orchestra, composed of musical friends with Maestro Ríos conducting, installed itself on a stage that looked like hell, and performed Afrocuban rhythms as semi-nude girls threw themselves into the Cocaine Dance, or a famous dancer named Tits of Sand organized dance contests for the aroused patrons.

In mid-1934 Miguel Hernández arrived in Madrid. Perhaps in this shy, poor young man coming to Madrid for the second time, Neruda saw something of his own life, of his arrival to Santiago from the south of Chile, with little more than hopes. He immediately gave him a warm welcome. Hernández was a private, solitary man, confused by the whirlwind of bohemia. He'd begun to write verses in his native town of Orihuela, shepherding the family flock of goats, a job imposed by his father which kept him from his studies at school. The previous year he'd published his first book, *Perito en lunas* [Expert in Moons], which had met with little praise. He'd arrived in Madrid prepared to work at any job in order to leave behind the limited opportunities of the land from which he'd come. Neruda brought him close to his poetic world and dissuaded him from other influences, seeking to save him from a Catholic way of thinking. "Your poetry smells like incense and sacristies," he once told him harshly.

Hernández received a controversial reception from the group at Casa de las Flores. Delia adopted him as a son and the poets accepted him as one of their own, but Federico was less explicit. Miguel had already asked him for help previously, in desperate letters that had received no reply. Acario Cotapos fled from him, believing that the young man from Orihuela showed all the signs of some disease.

In the magazine *Cruz y Raya*, Neruda found poetic work translating English authors into Spanish and publishing his own writing. At the Chilean embassy he had been assigned the title of Cultural Attaché, since Gabriela Mistral officiated as consul with Luis Enrique Délano as her assistant. In this new life, Neruda truly felt that his world had expanded, and little by little he went about distancing himself from his feelings of impotence and frustration. All things began to feel possible.

The political situation was entering a critical moment. The right, led by the government of Prime Minister Alejandro Lerroux, with the majority of Parliament in his favor, insisted on undoing what had been advanced by the Republicans, turning back reforms and naming to the key ministries of Agriculture, Work, and Justice three members of the most recalcitrant right-wing party, the CEDA (Spanish Confederation of Autonomous Rights). But this maneuver provoked an immediate reaction, with the declaration of a general strike that gained strength in Madrid and the provinces, especially Asturias, where the coal miners put up a tough resistance against the ruling class and press censorship that ended in a brutal massacre. The environment in Madrid was incredibly tense. Police, assault troops, and members of the feared Civil Guard patrolled the streets, walking behind groups of workers on strike whistling "The Internacionale". At night, exchanges of shots could be heard. The two sides were no longer able to find any possibility of agreement. Their visions were too opposed to be able to strike up a dialogue.

The Alliance of Intellectuals was on notice, since the right had emphatically rejected all the cultural applications sent by what they saw as Reds who wanted to spread their ideas through Spain with the money of the State. The La Barraca theater directed and created by García Lorca, which had traveled around the provinces to stage the Spanish classics, received the most furious attacks. Everything cultural was stained in red.

As she'd done before when faced with too many activities, the first thing Delia did was abandon her courses at the San Fernando Academy. She was learning watercolor, but the skill required for this technique demanded time she didn't have. Her work at the Alliance, about which she was passionate, her obligations to the Anfistora Theater and everything that bohemian life involved—once, suffering from the flu, she'd been dragged out of her house wrapped in shawls—left no room for her perpetually postponed, chronically uncertain vocation.

Her personal relationship with Pablo intensified with the birth of his first daughter, Malva Marina. The girl was born on the fourth of October, and after a few days the doctors detected grave anomalies which resulted in a terrible diagnosis: hydrocephaly, the product of an embryonic defect. Its visible sign was a swelling of the brain near the forehead. The joy of the birth quickly vanished, and the couple became even more estranged. Maruca spent hours shut away with her daughter, singing lullabies in Dutch. Neruda wrote poems inspired by the tragedy, sad poems for a new pain that had no remedy.

At the end of November, Victoria Ocampo arrived in Madrid to renew contact with contributors to the now successful magazine *Sur*. She visited María de Maeztu and Ortega y Gasset, to whom she owed the name of the magazine. Their relationship was complicated by sentimental confusion, although the philosopher's intellectual contributions remained important to her. Despite her friendship with Delia, their meeting did not go smoothly. Perhaps Delia wanted to hide her new love affair. She'd already made too much of a splash in Buenos Aires by joining the Communist Party to add a bohemian lifestyle to her reputation. She and Victoria were miles apart in their political views. Without being a conservative, Victoria was uncritical of nationalism, and she stayed in touch with many people of this tendency, more concerned with literary and personal value than with political beliefs.

At Carlos Morla's parties, Victoria met Neruda and Gabriela Mistral. The two women struck up a serious friendship. It couldn't have been otherwise, as both were convinced of their worth and wore their privileges with aplomb, taking great care with their words and opinions. Out of these meetings an epistolary friendship was born, which didn't stop even when Gabriela was Victoria's guest at her villa in San Isidro. There, in the mornings, a maid gathered in a tray the pages that both had written to each other in a display of intellectualism. Neruda, in contrast, felt intimidated and shy when faced with this "Mona Lisa of the pampa," as Ortega y Gasset referred to Victoria.

Days later they all met again at Morla's house, this time to listen to García Lorca reading his *Yerma*. The dramatic story of the infertile woman captivated them for over two hours. But once the stuffier part of the audience had left, Federico, forgetting the trance of his impressive reading, started on another of his comic numbers, featuring a small-town mass at dawn with roosters and hens inside the church, which Cotapos imitated, everything ending in a chaos of bursting fireworks set to a parody of Chilean music.

Yerma premiered on December 29, featuring a performance by Margarita Xirgú. The leading actress was known to be friends with the politician Manuel Azaña, who had just been freed from prison in Barcelona. Federico was afraid that in Madrid he was gambling with the prestige he'd worked so hard to earn in Argentina, and so the Correos Brewery group accompanied him to rehearsals to show their support.

On the day of the premiere, the Teatro Español was packed. The audience included distinguished intellectuals like Marañón and Unamuno, ambassadors and obviously many friends. "To Delia, with the oath of his twenty-eight years and the doubts of his Anfistora Theater Club," Federico wrote to her, in a dedication on her program. At the start of the performance, the gallery began to hiss in protest against Xirgu; eventually the protesters were expelled.

Despite the admiration of the public and the unanimous praise of critics, the magazines and newspapers of the right considered *Yerma* to be filth. They accused the author of being pagan, and his texts of exhibiting a blasphemously frank sensuality. Other publications made unambiguous allusions to the homosexuality of the author, a topic that his friends generally left alone.

The parties to celebrate the success of *Yerma* ended on the night of the New Year in 1935, at the Casa de las Flores.

Starting that year, Delia began to share a life with Neruda. Their relationship lost its secrecy as the poet shed his apprehensions and the Ant became his inseparable companion, as one can deduce from this letter addressed by Neruda to Adelina del Carril in Buenos Aires. He only knew of her through references and the letters to her sister:

> Dear Adelina, I have to send you many thanks for your letter, so understanding, so well-written and so crazy. I'm not very satisfied with these telegraphic restrictions, but Delia gave me a quarter of her peso and so I have to keep it short. All I have to tell you is how sympathetic you are, in the spiritual and the material. I always believe myself to be the one understood by that final allusion in your letters to Delia, 'Hugs to all those who love you', though the phrase is too small to fit me, since I adore Delia and cannot live without her. I have to scold her very often. A few days ago, when she was in charge of the kitchen for a few minutes, she brought us a soup of matches, since in her distraction after turning on the gas she'd thrown the matches in the pot. She loses her gloves inside all the streetcars, calls all the stocking sellers 'my son' and tries to pay on the bus with keys and buttons. You can tell me if she's just as she was, or has made progress. You delight me too, and even though I don't know you well enough I am prepared to adore you, and to fight with you a great deal over many things. Well, here we are, and we're not going to leave Delia. If you want to see her, come. Spain is so full of things that are blossoming

with simplicity, with simple life. Everywhere there are signs of personality and personal life, and one doesn't feel lost as in other places. Once again, thank you for your letter, which has so much supernatural froth and true heart. With all my friendship, Pablo Neruda. PS. Dear Adelina, let me take advantage of your goodness since I beg you to send these little messages to Oliverio and Molinari. Hugs, Pablo.

This letter, so full of naïve yet authentic sentiments, suggests the true nature of the relationship.

New accomplices arrived from Argentina: the poet Raúl González Tuñón and his wife Amparo Mom, who were old acquaintances of Delia's. The couples would become inseparable.

In a letter addressed to Héctor Eandi, an Argentine writer with whom Neruda had maintained a fluid correspondence during his stay in the East, in those difficult times when his book *Residence on Earth* couldn't find an editor, the poet spoke of his happy situation in Madrid: "I, who lived through an adolescence of vital roughness, am now convinced of the goodness in people." He added: "Delia del Carril, a very sympathetic and profoundly good Argentine woman, lives with us." This wasn't true; she never did live with them. He also gave another detail that didn't coincide with reality: "Right now she's having lunch with Victoria Ocampo, who is visiting Madrid." Victoria, at the date of the letter—January 1935—had already left Spain. Maybe these allusions were intended to impress Eandi with his new connections, to show that Neruda was putting the complaints and despondency of his past behind him. *Residence on Earth* had just been published in two volumes, in Cruz y Raya editions.

From Chile, Neruda received incredible attacks, completely opposed to the reception, flattery and recognition he received in

Spain. In Santiago, he seems to have unleashed a backlash against his triumphs. His rivals, the poets Pablo de Rokha and Vicente Huidobro, along with those close to them, initiated their attacks with virulence when it was discovered that the sixteenth poem of the *Twenty Love Poems* had an obvious resemblance, an unquestionable similarity, to one by the Indian poet Rabindranath Tagore in his book *The Gardener*. The explanations by Neruda, who by that time had already written so much that the accusation was ridiculous, didn't satisfy them. Headlines fueled the crusade, "Neruda, plagiarist or great poet?", "Neruda would be champion at the trick of plagiarizing poems" and "Unmasking Neruda, the poet of other people's verses".

In Madrid, Pablo prepared a brutal, lacerating, combative response. The subject wounded him at his weakest spot, exacerbating his fear of being exposed as having twisted intentions. The attacks transformed him into a vengeful being, full of hate. Delia and Federico calmed him down. The Spanish poets, to restore the balance, paid him a tribute that was printed in April 1935 by Plutarco, José Bergamín's publishing house. It contained three poems by Neruda: *Entrada a la madera* [Entrance into Wood], *Apogeo del apio* [Apogee of Celery] and *Estatuto del vino* [Ordinance of Wine]. Those involved in the tribute—Rafael Alberti, Vicente Aleixandre, Manuel Altolaguirre, Luis Cernuda, Gerardo Diego, Federico García Lorca, Jorge Guillén, Miguel Hernández, Luis Rosales and others—gave him their forceful support.

Madrid continued to receive distinguished visitors, and the house of the Morla couple was always the venue for unofficial receptions. If there were musicians, Pablo skipped the event, since he didn't understand music and didn't enjoy it, but Delia would go, as she was a knowledgeable enthusiast. That year, the performers and composers included Francis Poulenc, a very young Yehudi

Menuhin, the Chilean Claudio Arrau, and Arthur Rubinstein. The host Carlos Morla took pride in Federico's attendance. But one could never know with him, as he often promised to come but didn't show up, and days later would appear with flowers and poems, or if he met Morla in the street, would simply hold out a handkerchief on the sidewalk, kneel down, and ask for forgiveness in this extravagant way.

In those months a few young poets led by Manuel Altolaguirre decided to create a new publication, another magazine. They asked Neruda to be its editor. This is how *Caballo verde de la poesía* [Green Horse of Poetry] was born. In its pages new poems appeared by Miguel Hernández and Neruda himself, with Vicente Aleixandre also collaborating. The publication did not escape the ironic attacks of Juan Ramón Jiménez.

Vicente Aleixandre's attitude was very different. In his writings he recalled his outings with Delia, Pablo and Miguel Hernández—great walks through the Moncloa countryside near his house, with Miguel surprising them by climbing the trees and perfectly imitating the songs of a thousand different birds, the product of his observations from his time as a goatherd. Aleixandre and Neruda strongly influenced the deep change in Hernández's poetry. They shared a concern for the fate of the young poet, who still split his time between Madrid and Orihuela.

Federico García Lorca had achieved what he wanted, recognition in Spain as a theatrical author. Performances of his works followed. As he distanced himself from the management of La Barraca to reduce the political problems the tours provoked, he drew closer to the less dangerous Anfistora Club. But fame was tricky. In addition to being in the crosshairs of the groups on the right, he discovered that people were taking advantage of his work. For example, a young professor from the San Fernando Academy, a great admirer of his named Laínez Alcalá, was giving readings of poetry at night at the Granja del Enar café which included his verses, to the accompaniment of guitar. Aghast at the very idea, Lorca asked his friends to go with him to see what it was all about. There was the young man reciting his verses, giving them a sing-song rhythm. Outraged, Lorca stopped the event and furiously accused Alcalá of being tasteless and absurd. "Let's see if next time you start to read Joyce accompanied by a drum," he shouted as he left.

In November a scandal exploded that had consequences for Neruda. On October 2, 1935 a very private letter from Gabriela Mistral to her friend Armando Donoso was published in the magazine *La Familia*, in Santiago de Chile. The Spanish in Chile felt insulted, and raised an outcry. Everything was amplified by the perception that it was the consul who had humiliated them. From the Ministry of Foreign Affairs, the complaint bounced back to the Embassy of Chile in Madrid. The transfer was immediate. Gabriela received strict orders to move to Portugal in under forty-eight hours. Without managing to say goodbye to anybody, she left by train to Lisbon with her Mexican friend Palma Guillén, with whom she lived. Neruda was named consul in Madrid, and he confirmed Luis Enrique Délano as his assistant.

The letter appeared in the final chapter of a series called *Vida y confidencias de Gabriela Mistral* [Life and Secrets of Gabriela Mistral], written by the journalist Miguel Munizaga Irribarren. In the previous chapters, there were laudatory references to Gabriela. It's very hard to imagine that the publication intended to harm her. Maybe the journalist didn't weigh the consequences.

Here is the famous letter always mentioned:

I still don't know if I should tell you about my real Spain, or if I should leave you with yours. Ay, they are so different! You see a land of writers, while here in the country itself, I consider that much less than the common people.

For two years I have lived in the midst of an indecipherable people, full of contradictions and an absurd level of fraud that is even impressive, but all the same pure absurdity. Starving and without the strength to do themselves justice, illiterate as the neighboring Arabs (such an unfortunate caste), disjointed, today Republican, tomorrow monarchist supporters of Felipe González, a people with scorn and hate for everybody else: for France, for England, for Italy, for America… which they call Spanish. Envious because they're unhappy, for no other reason. I don't know if they are lazy, as the European world says, but they're disorganized to the point that one doesn't know what to say. A people with awful schooling and a pretty and amusing way of speaking, a people without the most basic hygiene, without doctors, without a salary to provide medical treatment for a daughter or wife. They care little or nothing about having a house, clothes, enough food. At the same time, the Spaniard has another image, and men of letters build illusions about him based on the classic picture cards; they call him stoic because of how much he's able to bear, or happy due to the genuine green-happy language of the Andalusian and the Basque. But when were the Basque ever Spanish? They can say he's a gentleman, for he conserves, in some behaviors and even his features, traces of what he once was, the owner of the world. They can call him strong, since hunger doesn't destroy him, and even in the trash of the city, one can find three calamities to eat. Ay, it hurts in the heart, as Unamuno says of this wounded and starving Spain. And it hurts because we used to be theirs and it isn't in vain that one carries a body in Spanish grams. But those South American intellectuals and pseudo-intellectuals who send off little articles or shout at the top of their lungs that we should become Spanish are delirious. Or is it Spanish politics that they'd like to import, as if our tragedy were small enough that we could double it with Hispanic influence, at this bruised hour for Spain? They don't have any conscience or decorum to shout this way.

I arrived at the height of the Azaña government. He was a great man, worthy of the best race in Europe, and in his writings he seems to be a Roman from the period of glory (in his speeches I mean), with essays worthy of the great Spaniards from whatever period you like. Governing with him were the Ríos, the Domingos, and others from the line that went to America to teach us democracy. Azaña didn't steal or persecute, but promoted intellectuals and filled the administration with well-read, informed people. Unlike him they didn't do anything of worth; they didn't do anything at all.

They were and are just as Spanish as all the rest. That is, their Asian squalor, their national Asian filth, the tragic strike of their workers, the dispossession of the peasant from the earth, seem more or less natural to them. And they have the same tired rhythm of life as the others and the same dark internal fanaticism and the same contempt for justice. Naturally you've heard about the great agrarian laws and the fabulous creations of schools and the perfect labor reforms. They didn't apply them, they didn't enforce them, they didn't hammer them in. They're flabby, spineless people, big talkers, fond of showing off. They don't serve the people. Ah, what for!, they said, and left it exactly the same. The reaction came. You know already: the Spanish womenfolk—without redemption and without names—voted according to their ignorance and their foolishness, which isn't only ignorance. They voted for the right wing as a block. And the deceived and stupid peasants did the same. The lack of intelligence in the womenfolk and peasantry is fantastic; they seem to be creatures of the tribe. Since the Spaniard likes to appear, since he doesn't have the will to be, the President brought Lerroux to cover the republic as a mantle, to give the semblance of a liberal center to some governments of the absolute stinking right, of the most obvious monarchist kind. As far as what is coming, it will be a few more degrees of conservatism, that is, Spain as usual: without looking toward the century nor toward Europe, closed to all democracy, limp, weak, the mother of privilege, the producer of the soldier and priest down to the infinitely lowest level.

Today, as we all know, we have the communists and the anarchists (socialism is a fib), but there aren't enough communists to triumph against an enormous police force; and the anarchists strictly correspond to the most classic Spanish type: they hate organization, and no government, good or bad, matters to them. One area is de facto separate, Catalonia and part of the Basque Country. The Catalan has made a country taking the French as an example; he has created a great industry; he has his wits about him, he is lively, he has turned his back on the tomb of Castile, and he has cultivated the sea, trade, the Greek and Latin classics, and a regional spirit amongst the wisest and most marvelous in Europe. It isn't that they're separatists, it's that they've always been another race, with another rhythm, another sense of life. Catholicism is still present. The famous Andalusian is an idol that has no surname because he's so much older than any other. Spanish is a superficial covering over the feudal regime—subfeudalism without an ideology—and ancient tyranny. I haven't seen the Basque up close. Fascism: it would be Spanish if it arrived, and this says it all.

Coming to Spain from America means learning the language. We don't know it, and this is a shame we carry. We come here and see the Prado and the rest of the museums with big paintings. Then we leave. Spanish life is bitter, naked, dry, very poor, and sad for one who doesn't live inside cafés, drunk on big talks, silly, filling the air with incense so as not to see apathy and blurring the tragedy of the country with cigarette smoke. I don't like bullfighting, I can't bear cafés, the squalor of the people doesn't matter to me, the lie of the new patriotisms disgusts me, and I believe that politics is economics and nothing else. I live here in great unhappiness, without any joy, burdened with idle visits that don't let me work, listening to idiocies about Jacobin or sacristan politics, in a poor climate that has increased my rheumatism and arterial pressure. I don't know what I'm doing here.

There's a young, very refined, elite generation, more of a daughter to English poetry and the English, German or Spanish essay. I like it almost entirely. These young people—but only the youngest—have undertaken within themselves a reformation of this Spain in rags, with a universal fury. They're often chivalrous and have a spiritual streak, with internal and external principles. But there are too few of them to remake a race. Many of them feel their tragedy.

Apart from the immediate distancing of the consul, the Spanish intellectuals did not add to the scandal unleashed by the letter's publication. All the same, during the meetings of the Pen Club, which took place at the Ritz Hotel, the name "Gabriela" was often heard in conversations with furrowed brows and shaking heads. Mistral, who often committed the sin of frankness, always considered herself to be a victim of persecution, betrayed and misunderstood.

Neruda set up the consulate in his own home, knocking down walls and widening the office that doubled as a living room, where he began to gather his purchases of first-edition books and hang up his masks from the East, along with other peculiarities that he'd gone about selecting during his strolls through the Rastro. In the same way, he also made the place more spacious for group meetings, which continued to occur at night despite complaints from the neighbors, who once even arrived with shotguns to demand silence when the revelry became truly diabolical.

Delia invited everyone to spend the Christmas of '35 at her house, in her apartment on Goya Street. She entrusted the task of buying a turkey to Isaías Cabezón. The truth is that Delia really only provided the house and the goodwill of Josefa; the guests had to take responsibility for all the practical details. It would have been enough to serve a cup of cognac, as had been announced, but the variety of alcohol was far greater. The turkey, held by the painter Cabezón, made an outing around the bars before its sacrifice. Due to its size, the dead turkey needed to be sent to a bakery for cooking, and took a very long time because of its age. The meal started at dawn. None of this affected the owner of the house, who always said that the important thing was to get together and converse, thus liberating herself from any obligations.

So as not to repeat these complications, they celebrated New Year's Eve in the street amidst thousands of Madrid natives, participating in all the local rituals.

The political situation was highly strained, and another confrontation took place at the ballot box. A new election at the Courts was called for February 16, 1936. The Republican forces weren't prepared for another defeat, so they signed a new pact to form a Popular Front. Only the anarchists were excluded.

When Alberti and María Teresa León returned from long trips through the United States and Russia, over a hundred intellectuals attended a meal in their honor at the Café Nacional. The whole group was there, of course, and Federico García Lorca gave a reading of his *Los intelectuales con el bloque popular* [The Intellectuals with the Popular Bloc], a fervent call for a commitment to democracy. There were only a few days until the election, and the atmosphere in Madrid, in all of Spain, was tense.

The triumph of the Popular Front by a slim but clear majority ignited enthusiasm in the streets. There were tremendous festivities at the Casa de las Flores as the poets celebrated the victory.

In May, the Courts dismissed President Alcalá Zamora and replaced him with the leader of the Republican left, Manuel Azaña.

As usual, despite all the stumbling blocks and the anxiety of the political climate, daily life found a way to continue through the worst omens, the nocturnal gunfights, the warnings and rumors, the clear animosity between the increasingly brutal factions, the street fights, and the drastic divisions of families. Ideologies began to take precedence over relationships and friendships, and even though it was obvious that something had to explode, since if things continued this way they could only end in a furious anarchy, even so everybody went on with their own affairs. Delia kept going to the Anfistora Theater, preparing for a premiere of Ramón del Valle Inclán's *Los cuernos de don Friolera* [The Horns of Don Friolera]; Neruda progressed with his work for the consulate and magazine; Lorca made corrections to his latest work, *La casa de*

Bernarda Alba [The House of Bernarda Alba]; the Morla couple arranged their social gatherings, receiving new artists who arrived in Madrid; and Luis Enrique Délano and Lola Falcón had their first son, whom they'd called "Polycarp" during the pregnancy, but in official papers registered as Enrique.

The Délano couple had moved to Rodríguez San Pedro Street in the Argüelles neighborhood, closer to the consulate. During a short trip to Portugal, Luis Enrique Délano made spoken arrangements to rent a little house in Gascaes for the summer, by Pablo's request. At first temporarily while they were away on this trip, and then staying on because of the tumultuous situation in the city, Delia left her apartment and went to live with the Délano couple. Pablo visited her there. One night when got home, he realized that he'd lost his keys. They were found in Delia's bed, but even with this evidence, the owners of the house didn't suspect them of having anything more than a tight intellectual friendship.

With things in Madrid as they were, and with his new love in mind, Neruda convinced Maruca to go with their daughter to Barcelona, where she would be received by the Consul General Tulio Maquieira, who was moved by Malva Marina's illness and the danger of her staying in Madrid.

But the famous summer holiday to Portugal, much desired and long planned, was not to be.

On July 12 the deputy José Castillo, a figure on the left, was assassinated. The next day, the leader of the monarchists, José Calvo Sotelo, disappeared, and was found dead that same afternoon with a gunshot to the back of the neck.

That night, Delia and Pablo, Manolo Altolaguirre, Luis Cernuda and several others ate at the Morla couples' home. The topic was of course the consequences of these two crimes. The murder of Calvo Sotelo produced unanticipated reactions. Delia vehemently commented that it was a crime committed by the fascists themselves to blame the Republicans, in order to find a convincing excuse for a total uprising. Carlos Morla considered this to be an outrageous exaggeration.

Through comments like these, her loyalty to the party and her impressively up-to-date information, the Ant gained another nickname amongst her friends: "the Eye of Molotov", a reference to the Soviet politician faithful to Stalin, who was then the leader of the Soviet Union.

Calvo Sotelo's murder was a reaction to the crime committed by the Falangists against José Castillo, a man beloved by the soldiers of the Assault Guard, who had taken their revenge.

But the reaction of the right was forceful and immediate. On the night of July 17, the Spanish army in Africa rebelled, led by General Emilio Mola, who together with General José Sanjurjo had prepared and designed the military coup that gave rise to the civil war. Sanjurjo had an aviation accident on July 18 that cost him his life, and only then did Francisco Franco come to shape the rebellion. He was named as Generalissimo of the army and Head of State. He was known to have directed the brutal repression against the miners of Asturias in 1934. The next year Emilio Mola also died, in another plane crash.

The military revolt didn't have the strength to seize power in the entire country. Spain remained divided between the rebel forces and the Republicans as a trench war began on the outskirts of Madrid. The city would be a symbol of victory for whoever dominated it.

After so many years of political tension, the accumulated tension burst open into armed conflict. Overnight the city was at war. Workers with firearms, green helmets and blue overalls, the uniform improvised by the republicans, went to the front in trucks, with shouts and songs that echo to this day. The streets received a battering from aerial attacks, and daily life became dangerous and difficult. Shots and more shots were heard from morning to night, from the rooftops and fascist houses. Republicans were ambushed by the pro-Franco groups that appeared in the city. There were serious problems regarding limited provisions, the persecution of nobles, the takeover of houses and palaces, and attacks on churches; but despite the chaos the people were roused and prepared for anything, knowing that the outskirts of Madrid had been captured by the opposing army, which reduced the matter to life or death.

In the palace abandoned by the marquises of Heredia Spinola, at 7 Marqués del Duero street, the Alliance of Intellectuals set up camp. To their surprise, in the wardrobes belonging to the owner of the house, they found 1,200 shirts, 600 pairs of shoes and 450 suits, which passed into the possession of the International Red Aid. Many artists went to live there. Acario Cotapos had the rooms of the marchioness, and he entrenched himself inside, hoarding bottles of water in his growing panic about germs. He felt very sick; he didn't know that the waters of Carabaña and Loeches, which he'd got hold of, are purgative. María Teresa León, dying with laughter, saved him from the illness that he claimed made him feel close to the grave. Acario, in blue overalls like a good soldier, stood guard at the doors of the palace, and every now and then climbed into a truck to go to the front. One day the truck was attacked, and Acario fell to the ground. He felt a liquid on his face, and thought: "I am wounded." Quickly he discovered that it was a great gob of spit from the street. This terrified him even more than blood and bullets. He would have preferred to have been badly hurt, as he told everyone who couldn't stop laughing at his adventures. At night they got together to eat at the palace, improvising meals with lentils that had arrived as aid from Mexico. When the marquises had fled from the palace, they'd left behind an impressive collection of suits, capes and hats with plumes and feathers, which were used to end the night in costume. Humor and celebrations were not set aside despite the state of war.

The Chilean embassy was crowded with refugees. They arrived in increasing numbers, and during the war years more than two thousand were recorded. Dukes, marquises, nuns, priests and aristocrats of every kind appeared, terrified by the mobs that wanted to lynch them, and convinced that Generalissimo Franco would appear at any moment to save them. Carlos Morla's house transformed into a shelter for his noble friends, and there was no longer any space for social gatherings. The Chilean government, with President Arturo Alessandri Palma at its head, was undoubtedly on Franco's side, and it gave asylum and leased many houses under the flag of Chile.

In the first days of September, the death of Federico García Lorca appeared in the newspapers. Disbelief and helplessness gave way to certainty. A few days after the assassination, in the middle of August, the news of the death of Jacinto Benavente at the hands of the Republicans also appeared in right-wing newspapers. The falsity of this account was a maneuver intended to justify the true crime that had already been committed.

In the midst of such danger and so many threats, the precise and deliberate death of one of the men whom nobody could imagine dead—for if anyone was joyfully full of life, it was Federico—produced a brutal sadness in the group, the feeling of a deep internal collapse. The war showed its most serious and horrifying face. One saw it in the street everyday, but this news was too much. Now anything was possible.

When had they seen him for the last time? Two days before leaving for Granada without notice, on someone's advice, scared of the situation, at the Casa de las Flores eating a gazpacho, his last one.

The stories of his death were all gruesome, claiming that he'd said: "Kill me, please, kill me already" to his executioners in the Black Squad of the Falangists. Or claiming that it had been at the barracks of Granada, or that they'd pushed him out during one of those terrifying drives, when people were forced out of the car and riddled with bullets for a supposed escape attempt down a nearby road. Or claiming that they'd told him atrocious, humiliating things, that they'd killed him for being a fag and a Red. With the crime revealed, the extent of the brutal repression that had been unleashed in Granada at the hands of the fascist rebels now became clear in Madrid.

If at the start it had seemed unbelievable, the news of people who fled from Granada and ended up at the Alliance confirmed how and where it had happened. Everybody cried, so many times, and cried again, so many years later, remembering those days and that death.

For Neruda, the harsh reality moved him to commit himself increasingly to the Republican cause, forgetting the tact that his post demanded. His natural tendency was to move closer to communist ideas with determination. By his side he had Delia, a believer, and Rafael Alberti, who went on repeating that the death of Federico was his death, that they'd made an error, that the death had been meant for him. And there was González Tuñón, another fervent militant. Another space thus opened up in his poetry, which had previously always been rooted in personal events. Now his subjects expanded to the suffering of war, and to the struggle of the armed Spanish people.

Thus the previous words of the poet were buried, the ones that he'd written to Héctor Eandi from Santiago de Chile in February 1933:

> A wave of Marxism seems to be taking over the world, and the letters that reach me from Chilean friends harass me toward this position. The reality, politically, is that one can no longer be anything but a communist or an anti-communist... I still feel the mistrust of the anarchist toward the forms of state, toward impure politics. But I believe that my point of view as a romantic intellectual has no importance. One thing is true, however. I hate proletarian, proletarianizing art. Systematic art cannot tempt, no matter the period, anyone but the artist of the least significance. Here there is an invasion of odes to Moscow, armored trains, etc. I go on writing about dreams...

The Ant, the Eye of Molotov, was his companion and adviser in this unfamiliar terrain, as well as the first sharp and meticulous reader of his writings, pointing out errors and approving changes, with the painstaking care and insistence which she put into all subjects that interested her.

Much has been said of the fundamental role Delia played in this period, of the transcendental significance of this sentimental encounter for the future of Neruda, which went beyond the romantic, extending to his professional work and public life. This is true, but there are no precise events, causes and consequences. It was something subtle that emerged and was maintained by their daily co-existence. Years later she would say: "I don't remember it myself. You know, I'll have to think about what I was doing at the time."

The situation in Madrid was unbearable. Battles and bombings made the streets impassable. In vast areas, after the attacks, only the façades of houses remained, their interiors destroyed, amidst rubble, abandoned bodies, stains of dry blood on paving stones, enormous holes in the bullet-ridden walls and a devastating silence. So that the destruction would not be total, major monuments were covered with bags of sand, and the most famous fountains and statues were protected. People referred to La Cibeles as "the pretty covered girl"; some humor still remained in the midst of so much disaster.

Nights were the worst, full of silence and darkness, the lights turned out in the streets and houses so as not to present a target for enemy planes sent from Hitler's Germany. At those hours, the women faced all kinds of dangers as they tried to put food in the mouths of their families, while the men came and went from the battlefront.

At that time Miguel Hernández returned to Madrid from Orihuela, ignoring the advice of his friends about the dangers they saw coming, and the hunt that had begun against intellectuals.

On September 18, a national holiday in Chile, was spent in darkness. Delia and Pablo, Luis Enrique Délano and Lola Falcón were at the Casa de las Flores, so close to the clamor of battle that the bullets could be heard whistling in the darkness from inside the house. The danger of going out was so great that they decided to spend the night there. But Delia didn't sleep with Pablo. "It seems that they still needed to pretend in front of us," says Lola.

Matters at the embassy were growing complicated. The ambassador Núñez Morgado was delighted by so much aristocracy and nobility around him, but panicked with "the Red mobs", as he called them. He only wanted to escape Madrid. This he soon did, leaving everything in the hands of Carlos Morla, but first he dismissed the consul for his impertinence and his commitments to the Republicans.

Franco's arrival at the outskirts of Madrid, and the increasing frequency of the battles, made Neruda and Délano decide to leave the city. On November 7, they departed the embassy in a car, with only what they were wearing. There wasn't space for anybody else. The women, Lola and Delia, put on several dresses, one over the other. Delia remained in Valencia, where several members of the Alliance of Intellectuals were helping to set up the republican government. The others continued toward Barcelona.

This meant a forced separation. Maruca was in Barcelona, and Neruda had to make a decision. A stage of life was ending. It had been both happy and tragic. But the certainty of his marriage had been left behind, since the physical separation encouraged speculation and doubt.

Can one trust the word of a poet? Amparo Mom had left for Buenos Aires because of problems with her husband, González Tuñón. Delia thought that she should go too, since she'd been told her mother was seriously ill, but what she was living through was more intense. She knew that her relationship with Neruda was the most important thing in her life, and that she must try to consolidate it. Pablo left for France. She communicated to him that she might stay in Spain and wanted to settle in Barcelona, that the situation was extraordinary and she should be there. Alone, in Valencia, all her doubts began to haunt her.

At the end of December, everything became clear. Neruda wrote to her from Marseilles, where he had gone to see the Délano couple embark on the Italian steamer *Virgilio* toward Chile.

Darling ant: I don't know why you're going to stay for months in Barcelona. You had plans. I left Maruca. The situation is arranged for her return. I'm in a very old hotel by the port. Every morning I watch the sailboats. Wouldn't it be wonderful if we were together! I hug you with my whole heart and love you every day. I hope to see you, it's the only thing I want. Pablo

The letter came with an unusual request: that she buy him a little boat he'd seen in a shop in Barcelona. This was the first request of many that Neruda would make of Delia, and he would ask similar things of other friends. He had the madness of the collector, a necessity to possess things, easily understandable given the hardships of his past. While he wanted to have everything, she scorned anything material that didn't interest her. But she humored this whim of Neruda's; he liked his little toys.

So she left for Barcelona radiant and happy, and made the poet León Felipe go with her to look for Pablo's sailboat. As soon as she had it, she left for Paris.

CHAPTER 7

1937

This Paris was different now after the experience of three years in Spain, which had changed her life in so many ways. She had gone on a great adventure, finding everything that she hadn't achieved in life before, a cause as well as love. She settled with Pablo into a seedy hotel. She didn't want to knock on the doors of old friends or acquaintances, in a city that had known a different Delia del Carril than the one who was arriving now. But a sad piece of news was waiting for her. Her mother, Julia Iraeta, had died in Buenos Aires, the victim of pancreatic cancer. On January 18, 1937, Delia sent this letter to Buenos Aires:

> Dear Amparo (Mom), Victoria (Ocampo) and Adelina: The death of my poor dear mother Julia has affected me as I would never have believed, despite everything. Despite knowing it, despite expecting it, despite being aware of what had to happen. It's taken away the little desire I had to go to Bs. As., although it seems necessary for me to do so. Lebretón received

me very affectionately and protested when I asked for repatriation in third class. 'My offer is for you to go in first, but if you, Madame, want to look foolish, go in the class you wish, taking into account that I will write to Bs. As. to say I have offered for you to travel in the best conditions.'

I was left horrified by the idiocy of the human race, and by the class of people that calls itself cultured, educated and Catholic.

Lebretón and the daughter of Drago and Sarita Castillo have told me the absurd and tremendous things being said about me. Tota (Atucha) tells me that in Bs. As. the crude fabrication circulates that I wrote a letter about how I went out at night to hunt fascists—it was very easy to demonstrate the falsehood with the text of my letters themselves—but what's said about me doesn't matter to me in the slightest. Such slanders and coarse insults are attributed to the Spanish people despite the testimonies of all the rest of us who have seen things, neutral foreigners like the English members of Parliament, English journalists, even those on the newspapers of the French right such as that poor Delapreé who died on the French embassy plane—along with all the others who were in Madrid with our hearts clenched tight, hoping for the luck of Madrid and the Spanish people.

May I never speak with a French person again, because even the people I've loved there have their premade ideas, unshakeable and riveted with pure lies. From you, Victoria, even from Elena Hurtado who said: 'Your French friends told me you're a communist.' The incomprehension and lack of culture of all these people is nothing beside their moral baseness, and they make one understand the necessity for war and revolution. I, who am incapable of killing anyone, when I see a friend wrapped in slander would leap up to strangle the swine responsible, and for my part I'll say that more than ever, I'm speaking what I think, proud of my words, with a total absence of egoism and no personal advantage.

I feel completely lost outside of Spain. I haven't even determined the date of my trip yet, anxious as I am about what's happening in Madrid. I'd like to receive a letter from you, Victoria. It seems strange to me that I've had no direct contact with you for so long. We have so much to talk about that it doesn't fit into letters anymore. Amparito darling, write to me at 7 Rue Belloni, chez Mr. Vargas, Paris XIV.

Pablo will give a conference on Federico García Lorca on the 20th—he greatly wishes that you would all to write to him.

It's incredible how to those of us who came from Spain (Pablo, Bergantín, Luis Lacasa), Paris seems to be living a retrospective life—behind by fifty years. The French get a little offended at this, but it's the truth. I've read Leo Ferrero's diary in the latest issue of *Sur*, and think of all the vulgar comments that this will bring to Victoria. In contrast, Gide's book is now wielded by fascists as a weapon against not just Russia, but against every noble and disinterested idea in favor of the class that works and builds the world.

Adelina, what are your plans? What are my brothers doing? Hug them with all my heart and all my tenderness that mourns for our dear mother Julia.

I am living as austerely as possible because I left Madrid with what I was wearing, and in France everything is extremely expensive. Kisses and lots of affection for N. and N. and N. All of you, please write to me. I am very sad. Delia.

Since she was informed about this death from a distance, it didn't have the same impact as if she had been there at the final moments, present for the process of seeing the corpse and attending the burial; it left behind an underlying feeling that none of it was true. Having taken place so far away, there was no evidence that this triggered memories for Delia, or the guilt of a distant and tense relationship that despite the discretion of silence, involved Julia Iraeta's tacit disapproval of her daughter's unpredictable life. Delia's references to the French in this letter were the consequence of the political situation in the country.

The victory of the Popular Front in the French elections of 1935 had brought the Jewish intellectual Léon Blum to power as Fascism and Nazism made their way in the neighboring countries, suggesting an escape and a saving grace for the Spanish Republic. But this was not the case. The pressures from the right and from Spain's natural ally at that moment, England, forced Blum to declare his total neutrality, ignoring agreements of commercial exchange that included arms, and blocking part of the gold reserve that the Republicans had deposited in France to safeguard against disaster.

In parallel, a network of intellectuals committed to antifascism was growing, financed by Moscow, supported by Stalin, and devised by one of the founders of the German communist party, Willy Münzenberg, the France-based head of western propaganda for the Komintern. Under this organizational wing, non-communist and communist artists joined in the defense of culture and peace against the fascist threat. Their headquarters was in Paris, and their center of operations was on the left bank of the Seine. Intellectuals and artist lived close together near the already legendary cafés of Saint-Germain-des-Prés and Montparnasse. La Coupole, Les Deux Magots and the Café de Flore became gathering places for political strategizing. Delia introduced Pablo to the circles of Louis Aragon and Paul Éluard, their closest friends

Image courtesy Pablo Neruda Foundation

Delia and Pablo at Isla Negra, 1946.

in the city. Through Aragon, Neruda got a job with the Association for the Defense of Culture. It paid paltry wages, but at least it offered a salary for someone who had been left unemployed after the annulment of his consulship. In the meantime, the couple lived off Delia's property income, which always arrived from Buenos Aires after a delay. She was no longer a rich woman.

And here we enter into the delicate topic of money, about which Pablo Neruda was not very considerate. In his memoirs, *Confieso que he vivido* [*I Confess That I Have Lived*, translated into English as *Memoirs*], he traces a path through his life that includes unforgivable oversights, incredible omissions, and some hidden moments of revenge, such as in the paragraph about Adelina del Carril: "This lady was a theosophical and superficial woman, with no other passion than Asian philosophies, who lived in a remote village in India." His description of his first stay in Paris is very brief: "I'd been left without the consulship and thus without a penny. I went to work, for four hundred old francs a month, at an association for the defense of culture managed by Aragon. Delia del Carril, my wife then and for many years afterward, was thought to be a rich landowner but the truth is that she was poorer than I was."

Without a doubt, Delia was not poorer than he was. Perhaps the poet wasn't aware that when someone comes from family as rich as the del Carrils were, something always remains: properties, plots of land, small incomes. But Neruda always protected himself from any suspicion that he took advantage of others. He successfully hid all the details that could cast a shadow on his merit, rather than accept with natural grace the help that seemed obvious under such conditions.

At the same time, María Antonieta Hagenaar and her ill daughter had moved to Montecarlo. Finding herself in desperate economic straits, María Antonieta wrote directly to the President of Chile, Arturo Alessandri Palma, asking him to reinstate Neruda as consul, citing their distressing situation and the intellectual merits of her husband. In a final appeal, she requested the repatriation of herself and their daughter to Chile as third-class passengers. Receiving no reply, and faced with Neruda's silence, she decided to leave with her daughter for the Netherlands, where her family lived.

For intellectuals, above all writers, enjoying the blessing of Moscow meant invitations to travel through the Soviet Union, publish their books there and receive enormous benefits. Print runs of four hundred thousand copies or more were something that everyone hoped to achieve. Moscow selected its grant winners with pincers, calculating the value and weight each choice would yield in terms of prestige and good publicity in the west.

For this reason, André Gide's reaction after a trip to Moscow created a scandal. Gide had been invited there after declaring his sympathies for the Soviet system, and had been given the offer to be published and see up-close the incredible benefits of the new social organization. When he published *Return from the USSR* in the last days of 1936, the book fell like a bomb. Not only did it give an account of a system in which an extremely poor class continued to face flagrant injustices, but it also described how culture and freedom were subordinate to the State, which passed legislation strictly governing the moral behavior of its citizens.

Accused of being a traitor, of focusing on these topics when the antifascist struggle at stake in the world was of greater importance, Gide was erased from all the intellectual committees and attacked in newspapers and political meetings. Nor did he hear any applause from the conservative side. He was left isolated. In Paris, his book made no impression on the followers of communism.

Preparations continued for a new Congress of Intellectuals with headquarters in Madrid, although given the circumstances of the civil war, the destination was moved to Valencia, where the Republican government had been set up.

Plans were made for the congress to begin on July 4, 1937, and Delia and Pablo and Raúl González Tuñón and Amparo Mom, who had returned from Buenos Aires reconciled with her husband, worked hard to help prepare it. José Bergamín was the delegate for the Spanish and South American writers, and under his authority invitations were organized and means sought to gather the greatest number of well-known names possible, to help give cultural support to the collapsing Spanish Republic.

In these circumstances, Neruda gradually took a leading place among the invited writers, which allowed him a small revenge on Vicente Huidobro, the Chilean poet with whom he'd often engaged in literary disputes. Huidobro had come to France to attend the congress, even though he hadn't received an official invitation. He joined the nearly two hundred intellectuals who would meet in Valencia, but couldn't manage to oust Neruda from the preeminence that he had quickly achieved.

Delia didn't like Huidobro either, and not only because he was Pablo's enemy. She'd met him in Paris years before, when the poet had arrived with a new wife, a very young woman named Jimena Amunátegui, fleeing her family after the two eloped. They were together at a meal when Huidobro harshly told his wife to be quiet, and she started to cry in silence. "While she ate her soup"—Delia would recount later—"I saw the spoon return to its bowl full of liquid, her tears."

Surrounded by so many distinguished writers, with words of support from famous authors who had been unable to attend, the sentimental reunion of the group of friends from Madrid took place. Some were missing, above all Federico, but once again there were María Teresa León, Rafael Alberti, León Felipe, José Bergamín and Miguel Hernández. In his military uniform—he was enrolled in the Fifth Regiment—in the collective voice he had learned from his experience in the trenches, Hernández spoke: "Proletarian art, yes, but not the kind that gives alms to the poor. Let's cast aside the pitiful idea of the worker whom the intellectual offers a few very poor tablets of doctrine, leaving him on the margin of the advances produced in art during the first third of the twentieth century [...] To take an example, we can't admit that a painting is revolutionary, is genuine, due to the sole fact of its showing a worker with his fist raised, a red flag, or any other symbol that leaves the most essential reality unexpressed [...] The workers are more than simply good, strong, etc. They are men with passions, with suffering, with joys far more complex than these facile mechanical interpretations would have it [...] This explains our attitude to the art of propaganda. We don't deny its importance, but on its own, it seems insufficient." After three days in Valencia, the majority of the group traveled on to Madrid. Miguel accompanied Pablo and Delia to visit the Casa de las Flores, or what was left of this house of flowers: just a few collapsed walls and a lot of shrapnel amidst the debris.

Despite the warm welcome of the congress, the lovely words were of little use. The battles grew worse. Madrid's days were numbered. With nothing but weak support from the faraway Soviet Union, the republic ceded territory. It was cornered to the north. Any small victory was celebrated as a final triumph. "Something must be done for Spain" was the slogan, but reality can't be built with good wishes. Germany's support was forceful, and although it did not make any declarations of principles, it had more than enough airplanes.

The return to Paris, where the congress was ending in what appeared to be a defeat, made Neruda think that his only option was to return to Chile. Delia began her preparations, which consisted of reading history books, novels and poetry from the country. Their relationship had strengthened into love, and into a common effort. A world had suddenly opened up to them, with new relationships that made Pablo dream of more ambitious projects. In Spain he had glimpsed the halo, the graze, the scent of what is called fame, world fame, which had seemed impossible from Chile. He had to store up new strength, to return to his little country and his own small life, now accompanied by Delia, who had become his companion, correspondent and secretary, the woman who could pull a thousand relationships from her hat. She might not have had the slightest aptitude for reality, and she might have been forgetful, with a knack for losing things, but she had a real skill for knowing whom to contact. She never lost sight of what was convenient for Pablo.

CHAPTER 8

1938

Traveling by boat with Raúl González Tuñón and Amparo Mom, Delia and Pablo made their way to the port of Valparaíso. From there they took a train, arriving at Mapocho Station in Santiago on October 10, 1937.

Their closest friends were at the station. These were friends they'd met as children, in high school, or during bohemian Santiago nights. They were good companions for the hard times, when they were trying to catch a glimpse of the future, when the present was complicated by illusions of what was to come. Tomás Lago was there, who over ten years before had coauthored *Anillos* [Rings] with Neruda; so were his wife Irma Falcón, Diego Muñoz, Regina Falcón, Rubén Azocar, Lavinia Andrade and the unmistakable Acario Cotapos.

Delia was charming. She came down in a blue two-piece suit and a little pink hat. Someone would later say it was like an actress had appeared, because of her distant elegance, the quality of her clothing, and the wisps of blonde hair peeking out from under her hat. Such high style dazzled them.

"This is the Ant, say hello," Neruda introduced her.

The travelers settled into the City Hotel, and the same night attended a welcome party. There were many people, and the news of Delia's arrival spread among the guests, which included almost all of bohemian Santiago. Santiago was small, puny and provincial compared with other capitals.

The conversations centered especially on Pablo's arrival, and the new woman accompanying him. Much better for him. Just as well that he's left that Dutch lady, that unbearable woman. This one's charming. How old is she? No one knows. She's Argentine, very refined. Pablo's changed his hair, it's different, much better cared for. They say she's rich. From an Argentine family, extremely wealthy. Happy, the poet looks content. She's marvelous. So elegant. And so simple. You can see the change in the poet. Yes, it's for the best that he's left that Dutch lady.

The change was obvious, and Neruda was perpetually concerned about what was and wasn't said about him, as well as about others. He quickly brought himself up to date on the news from Santiago, both political and romantic, the latter of which interested him more. He liked to listen to the women, who gave him details about the latest events, quick marriages and courtships, making good use of the famous Chilean grapevine.

The Neruda and González Tuñón couples first settled into an apartment on Merced Street facing the Parque Forestal, then rented a big spacious house on Irarrázaval Avenue near Antonio Varas Street. This marked the start of an unusual way of life, with their doors always open to receive friends without restrictions. It quickly became clear that the Ant concerned herself only with issuing invitations. She would say to everyone she met: "Come

Delia with Pablo as he hides from arrest in Pirque, near Santiago, 1948.

over to the house, we're expecting you." It's likely that she quickly forgot, and was happily surprised when the guests appeared. Details had no importance for her, and things would arrange themselves on their own. But it meant that somebody had to take care of the rest. This is why Lavinia Andrade was such an indispensable housekeeper; in a very short time she could prepare food for a group of eighty. *Curantos* (seafood stews), *cazuelas* (heavy meat soups) and *corvinas* (sea bass), which Pablo bought from the market very early in the morning, were staple dishes. The parties weren't announced ahead of time, and no matter who arrived, there was enough for everyone. Such lavish display marked out a style.

Delia had changed Neruda's life. During his last stay in Santiago, after his return from the East, he'd lived with Maruca in a dark and narrow, inward-facing apartment on Catedral Street, facing the Congress building. No more than four people could fit into it. Tomás Lago and his wife Irma Falcón would show up there every morning; without Tomás the poet felt lost, and the two of them would go out all day long. Irma would stay behind with Maruca, or go for a walk with her without a single word being exchanged. Maruca refused to learn Spanish at first, and when she did pick up some, perhaps she felt shy about speaking it with others, in a new environment. In addition to her own worries, she needed to fulfill Neruda's requests and be with him at all times; she couldn't let him down. The poet's charm made it hard to refuse him, yet the relationship grew increasingly strained.

Without a doubt, things were different now. Delia was happily welcomed by Pablo's friends. If the del Carril family is from San Juan, and San Juan was once Chilean territory, then you're Chilean, they told her, an idea she found amusing. It was a way of approaching her, of cutting down the distance that separated them from this very different person, who belonged to a wider universe far removed from their simplicity. They didn't reckon on her ability to recognize a world and appropriate it, to meet new people and become a part of it in the most natural way.

THE ANT

Delia's enthusiasm about keeping the home open was also a
very subtle way of looking after Pablo. As in every relationship,
the tendencies of each went about creating strategies to achieve
a balance that ensured permanence. The poet needed his people,
and dispersion attracted him. His natural genius for poetry
and remarkable ease for unraveling words which perfectly represented what he was looking to say could be a double-edged
sword. And whether it was a pretense for her love or an honest
concern about her future, Delia applied a power that drew limits,
regulated schedules, avoided excesses. Neruda yielded. But this
authority pushed him to seek escape and look for alliances in
the game of appearing to give in without sacrificing too much
of his freedom. To say they formed a mother-son relationship
is too obvious. There was far greater complexity in this profound affection. They were twenty years apart, and everything
that they had learned in two dissimilar worlds colided. The Ant
was inflexible, and could be harsh. "Not that, Pablo, you're slow
in the head," was her battle phrase. And he arranged things to
make her uncomfortable for a moment, forcing a friend to tell a
crude joke or use a word with a vulgar meaning that drove her
up the wall. But this was just a part of their relationship. The two
also formed an affectionate, inseparable couple. They understood
each another. He was much more spontaneous, loving, warm and
concerned. Delia, educated that feelings should not be shown,
displayed a certain coldness, but her love expressed itself in an
unconditional loyalty, boundless support and total admiration.

The dominant environment in Santiago was prudish and
conservative, with all the characteristics of a small town. Yet the
Nerudian circle behaved with the looseness of those who don't
have to maintain appearances, distancing themselves from the
old asphyxiating structure. The traditional model demanded

submission, but didn't often accept or give opportunities to women, or most men from the provinces. Artists and writers were by vocation also marginalized from this formal world. They didn't belong to bourgeois families or have pretensions to set themselves up in this space; they lived in their own more liberated space, with the freedom not to be pigeonholed by restricting obstacles. Perhaps they looked to imitate the bohemia of other places. Whatever the case, the group served as a model in Chile.

Political questions were also being asked in that part of the world. The major newspapers had other heroes. Hitler and Mussolini were the salvation of a world that needed order and a firm hand. Franco was the leader of the moment.

Only a few newspapers on the left gave an account of the challenging situation faced by the Republicans. Neruda and González Tuñón gave conferences, and stirred up and inflamed the local conversation by talking about their experiences in the Spanish Civil War. Just as in Madrid and Paris, they formed a successful Alliance of Intellectuals, limiting it to a small group. They set up their offices in a little apartment at 15 Estado Street, on the third floor, transforming the space into a hive of men and women prepared to do something for the Spanish at the front and the many refugees in France who had been relegated to concentration camps.

The Alliance was a political cluster at the margins, another parallel world that served as a tool to unite and work for common ideals under the wing of the Communist Party.

In those days Delia decided to visit Buenos Aires to look after "her things", as she would say, so as not to talk about money. She also wanted to see her siblings, and to face the legend of her supposed life as a guerrilla fighter in Madrid. Things were the way they often are when someone goes away for many years. There had been changes. It was no longer possible to sell off floor by floor the building she owned on Garay Street, in Barrio Sur, and the lands that remained to her were still administrated by her family. Many scowled at her political ideas, but nobody dared mention the matter of the poet. She also took advantage of the moment to say goodbye to Adelina, who was leaving for India in search of the sources of Ricardo Güiraldes' spiritual philosophy.

In seven years of absence, too much had happened: marriages, new nephews and nieces, occasional economic setbacks that affected her. She learned that Adán Diehl, as expected, had gone bankrupt and given up the De Mallorca Hotel. He was now living in Buenos Aires. She gave power to a lawyer to process the divorce in Uruguay, finally putting an end to that bad memory.

During her short stay in Argentina, it became obvious that her life had taken a different path, diametrically opposed to the one that was expected in her country and family. After so many years away, she felt strange and unconnected to them, even if her feelings and affections persisted.

CHAPTER 9

1939–1943

In the midst of this flurry of political activity, the publisher Ercilla got in touch with Neruda to publish his books. For the sum of fifteen thousand pesos, it committed to reissuing his entire body of work. The author's condition was that *España en el Corazón* [Spain in the Heart] should be published before anything else. It included twenty-three poems born from his decisive experience of civil war. Two thousand copies were printed with illustrations by the painter Pedro Olmos. The book was translated in Paris, with a prologue by Louis Aragon, and it was the first publication of the International Association of Writers for the Defense of Culture. In Spain, as the war raged on, Manolo Altolaguirre also managed to publish an edition of the same book with the help of a few other militants, a situation that made the verses even more moving.

Neruda was already thinking of working on what would later be called the *Canto General*. In Santiago it was difficult to find moments of tranquility for his writing. The meetings at his house didn't stop, and the number of guests only continued to increase. Acario Cotapos had been received with open arms, and Delia loved him and celebrated his wisecracks. Neruda, who had no flair for telling jokes or stories, was an unconditional admirer of the musician's theatrical shows. Now included in his new repertoire were a few incredible sessions of the Chilean Congress, and in honor of Delia, a trip from Mendoza to Santiago in which he performed the different personalities of Argentines—high-flown and sassy—and Chileans—puny and timid—prolonging their entertainment until the early morning hours.

The political events also demanded a great deal of time. The organization of aid to the Spanish was joined to action through the candidacy of Pedro Aguirre Cerda for President of the Republic, representing the Popular Front formed by the left and the Radical Party. The right and its candidate Gustavo Ross were not going to give up power without a fight. Fear of a Red victory gave rise to a new campaign in which the worst and most terrible consequences were predicted if this came to pass. It went to the extreme of imagining cloistered nuns sent to the homes of family members after years of confinement to escape outrage, and suffering from fainting spells when confronted by a world with strange machines like automobiles. The campaign of the left warned against fascism and conservative abuse. In an electoral system where the wills of citizens were easily twisted with promises, ruses and threats, and the reigning government carried out its inspections with a full display of force, the chances of a popular triumph were slim. The right-wing machine seemed insurmountable.

Out of about five hundred thousand voters, a 4,111-vote margin gave the victory to the Popular Front. This wasn't a time to turn a blind eye to the counting process.

The Neruda couple celebrated the triumph with great festivities. The election allowed them to continue their plans to help thousands of Spanish refugees.

The government of Pedro Aguirre Cerda came into office on December 25, 1938, starting out cautiously to avoid handing a motive to the losers, alert to any opportunity that might favor them.

For this reason, the Communist Party didn't have a place in the makeup of the new ministry, and was relegated to a position of lesser importance.

In Chile and the world, events began to move quickly. An earthquake that devastated Chillán in January 1939 created an enormous display of solidarity throughout the country in which the Alliance of Intellectuals actively participated. But the situation in Spain became ever more pressing. President Aguirre Cerda accepted Neruda's proposal to bring the Spanish refugees from France to Chile, through an agreement with Louis Aragon and the Republican government in exile. Delia's activity was centered on getting hold of belongings and clothes for them; from a central office on Villavicencio Street, she collaborated with Doctor José Manuel Calvo and the Chilean committee to help the refugees in France. Amparo Mom, José Echeverría Yañez and Luis Enrique Délano also helped.

In March they left on another trip to Paris, this time to face an immense challenge. Before this, in Montevideo, they'd attended a meeting of Latin American countries against fascism. The official representative from Chile was Gabriel González Videla, who in a fiery speech appealed to the unity of Latin America against this danger.

In Paris the couple settled into a small apartment on the banks of the Seine at 45 Quai de L'Horloge, and immediately began

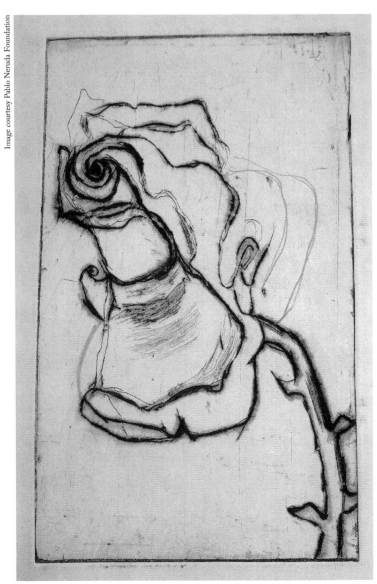

Engraving from the series *Historia de una rosa* [Story of a Rose], 1957.

work to transfer the Spanish refugees, who were spread out in different sites across the south of France. They didn't receive much support from the Chilean Embassy, which was far from eager to help the Spanish Republicans. In contrast, the Mexican Embassy nobly opened its doors, and French friends helped. The Republican government in exile, headed by the Spanish doctor Juan Negrín, was crucial in getting hold of the Canadian boat *Winnipeg*, which had previously transported cod and was now being prepared to move passengers.

The speed of the operation became urgent after the final triumph of Franco, who on May 19 celebrated his victory in Madrid with a military parade, in which Italians and Germans also participated. A hundred planes and two hundred thousand soldiers paraded before the Generalissimo for six hours under an incessant rain. Franco remained standing with his arm raised for the entire six hours.

The just-elected Pope Pius XII gave Franco his support, naming him Caudillo of the Faith.

Selecting from the thousands of refugees was difficult. The interests of the Spanish and the conveniences for Chile had to be balanced with the requests of professionals and specialists. And there were the requests of the refugees themselves, who learning of these preparations had fled from the concentration camps to Paris in order to ensure themselves a place.

Darío Carmona was among the first to arrive, and Neruda hired him as a secretary. Leopoldo Castedo, who had served as a journalist at the Congress in Valencia, also approached the apartment on the Quai de L'Horloge and found his place on the boat, while the young engineer Víctor Pey and his brother pleaded for their complete family, split up over different concentration camps.

Rafael Alberti and María Teresa León had arrived in Paris from a devastated Madrid and received the hospitality of the Neruda couple, staying at their apartment. They lived there until an Asturian, who had got hold of his place on the *Winnipeg*, could find no better token of gratitude than to sing at night, giving long serenades in honor of his saviors, heard for blocks surrounding. The landlady of the building asked them to leave, and they moved to other rooms that friends rented for them on Rue de Varennes.

From those days the legend of Delia's distraction emerges with greater force. Although she worked hard, concentrating on the selection and arrangement of the clothes that arrived in shipments from Chile and Argentina, on the day of the departure she had no head for matters. She painted her eyes with toothpaste, hung a couple of stockings on herself as a purse, and went out. Even worse, she made her way to the bank to pick up money, coming back with an empty envelope. Amusing, entertaining and airy is how Alberti remembered her from those days of living together.

But when the moment called for organization and work, she was capable. The day came to board the two thousand refugees who had arrived from Masonic lodges in Lyon, Quakers' shelters in Montpellier, and concentration camps, transferring to Bordeaux in crammed third-class trains without food or water. Family members who hadn't seen each other for months, and didn't know if they'd ever see each other again, now reunited. Impressive scenes took place in the midst of the wretched conditions. From there, the people were transferred to Pauillac and settled into the customs stalls, to proceed to their final inscription and embarkation at the dock of Trompeloupe, where the *Winnipeg* was berthed.

In two intense days of paperwork at a long table, Neruda and the representatives of the Republic took down information, resolving the last-minute appearances of family members who weren't on the lists. Delia kept busy with the distribution of dresses, shirts and shoes, as well as with arguments about the floral shirts that a few men rejected.

The women and children boarded in the cabins below, and the men in the ones above. Despite the uncomfortable little beds and the pervasive smell of cod, which the children from that time can still remember, they slept well because it was the final trip, their salvation.

The ex-refugees can also remember Delia and Pablo Neruda dressed in white, wearing hats to protect themselves from the fierce summer sun, lifting their arms to wave goodbye from the dock.

The *Winnipeg* arrived in Valparaíso on September 3, the same day that the world war was declared. At the port they were received by the Minister of Health, Salvador Allende. The next day they left for Santiago by train. Along the road there were greetings and flowers, and groups of people standing at even the smallest stations.

"The change couldn't have been more impressive. We, the execrable Reds, humiliated, dangerous, murderers, transformed into heroes of democracy, treated wonderfully, paid homage and cheered on by a crowd at Mapocho Station," one of the travelers recalls.

Delia and Pablo stayed in Paris for two months. Fear had begun to take hold in the city. At any moment they expected terrifying attacks in the night from the German air force, which had already tested the deadly bombardments in Spain it would now inflict over all of Europe.

The situation of the refugees at the Chilean Embassy in Madrid also worried the couple. They carried out procedures from France so Miguel Hernández would be included on the official list of refugees, reduced to seventeen men to whom the Franco government had refused asylum. It was an absurd figure compared with the thousands of Franco supporters Chile had sheltered in Madrid during the civil war. Hernández was arrested and then freed, but he refused to seek asylum because the birth of his second son was approaching. He was immediately put in jail again. The refugees, among them Santiago Ontañón, Pablo de la Fuente, Arturo Soria and Antonio Aparicio, could only leave Spain for Chile in 1941.

In January 1940 Delia and Pablo returned to Santiago. The poet wanted to dedicate himself to his work, to poetry, after the enormous effort of the operation of the *Winnipeg*. He needed a refuge, a place of calm where he wouldn't be harassed by friends.

A small notice in the newspaper about a house for sale on the coast attracted them. Delia visited Isla Negra, passing through the rural area of El Totoral. The country house was on the edge of the central coastal road, near the San Antonio port. The house itself was nothing to write home about, but it had the splendor of an incomparable view of the sea. Huge and continual waves diminished in size until they became transparent and crashed against the rocks with tremendous fury, dissolving onto thick shining sand filled with agate stones. There was also the strong smell, a mix of salt and iodine, of the Pacific Ocean, which was packed with seaweed and cochayuyo kelp. Completing the picture of this perfect place were a few inhabitants, sparse vegetation and a small community of intrepid fishermen, who went to the rocks to pull off sea urchins, abalones and crabs, and when the sea allowed it, climbed into barges to look for fish.

Delia bought the home under her name for thirty-five thousand pesos, from Eladio Sobrino, an ex-captain of the Merchant

Navy. The plot of land, around five thousand meters, was wide enough for the house to expand without any problem. The view of the sea was its only richness.

Refuge and solitude were a manner of speech. Friends slept in a spare bedroom and even in the hallway. The conditions were precarious, lighting came from paraffin lamps and murky water was drawn from a well. They purchased supplies from a small grocery store, El Piuchén. A young couple named Lucila and Florencio noted down their orders in books with black covers, to be paid at the end of each month. A humble boarding house on the banks of the Quebrada de Córdova, belonging to Doña Blanca, helped them out of a tight spot when visitors became numerous. But they were delighted with this simple life. They slept in a narrow bed pressed against a bay window where nearby the sea roared.

Around this time, an eccentric and outlandish millionaire Englishwoman named Nancy Cunard, whom they'd met in Madrid and Paris, docked in Chile. She had arrived in the company of her lover, a Spanish bullfighter, whom she had quickly left for a Chilean poet. Nancy easily adapted herself to the group's parties, adding a touch of madness to them and performing extravagant dances at Isla Negra in the moonlight, draped in cochayuyo kelp.

The *Winnipeg* operation, the conversations with French intellectuals and members of the Communist Party, and the shared life of political ideals they had envisaged since their meeting in Madrid created a solid link for the couple. It reinforced their relationship beyond the commitment of affection.

Delia's role was to support the poet in his work and his future. But this could become an unpleasant position. The conversation, the discussion, the analysis of an event often excited passions. In Chile her life took a turn with these friends and this permanent party where wine ran to excess and intimacies were often revealed she'd have preferred not to know. But Pablo encouraged these revelations, forcing her to keep at a distance. Sometimes she called for order, or put things in their place, playing the irritating role of a security guard. They didn't argue in public, and she expressed her annoyance by simply withdrawing, while he sneakily pretended not to notice, since he knew it had no greater significance.

Faced with such behavior, Delia went in search of allies, forming her own loyalties. Graciela Matte Hurtado, who participated in the Alliance of Intellectuals, gradually became her best friend, while Laurita Reyes, Neruda's sister, and Albertina Azócar, Neruda's girlfriend when they were younger and now the current wife of Ángel Cruchaga, stood by her in this impossible struggle for moderation.

The stay in Chile was brief. The government named Neruda as a consul to Mexico, and from Valparaíso they left for this country in the boat *Racuyo Man*. They went with Luis Enrique Délano, who'd also been appointed to a consulship there, and were joined by the complicated company of Nancy Cunard and her new poet boyfriend. He beat the Englishwoman so much during the journey that when they arrived in Manzanillo in August 1940, they had him arrested by the police.

In highly Nerudian style, Pablo fell in love with a strange-looking animal, a badger that delighted him with its teeth and incredible tail. He asked Luis Enrique to buy it for him as a gift, so he wouldn't have trouble with Delia and could avoid explanations. He knew that she'd say: "You're completely crazy, you're slow in the head."

The animal became the couples' pet and was given the name "the Child". The Child was lord and master of the houses where they lived in Mexico, and sowed panic amongst everyone except for its owners.

"He bites you because you make such a fuss when you see him, shouting and climbing on the sofas. It scares him," said Delia, coming to his defense.

They arrived in Mexico during the last days of the Lázaro Cárdenas government, which had made the country prosper and created a sense of order, paving the way for six-year terms dominated by the Institutional Revolutionary Party. Mexico lived in relative calm, while Europe was devastated by the German advances and the war reaching its peak.

Trotsky had just been assassinated. No doubt Stalin's power had extended to Coyoacán, the neighborhood where the exiled revolutionary had set up his general quarters. The anti-communist campaign intensified.

Neruda helped his friend David Alfaro Siqueiros, who had been arrested and accused of a previous unsuccessful assault on Trotsky's stronghold, by granting him a visa to Chile until it was safe to return. This unconsulted visa was one of the first problems between the poet and the Chilean government.

Despite the rivalries among intellectuals and artists, agitated by the eternal polemics between Siqueiros and Diego Rivera, the Neruda couple brought together people from all factions at their apartment on Revillagigedo and Independencia Street, inside a building in the purest Art Deco style. This group included Spanish friends, who were warmly received in the country with the unconditional support of President Cárdenas. Delia and Pablo reunited with their good friends from Madrid, León Felipe, José Bergamín, Emilio Prados and Wenceslao Roces, and they also received German and Italian émigrés. In those years Mexico was a country of exiles.

As in Chile, the house of the couple turned into a fortress for everybody. If Delia believed that Pablo's behavior would reform while abroad, she now had the palpable demonstration of the error of her expectations.

Every night was a party, a celebration. Tequila produced more euphoria than wine. One night the musician Silvestre Revueltas, who had become an intimate friend, arrived extremely drunk. He confused the badger with a duck and left the party, dramatically claiming that nobody loved him and that everyone's affection was for the duck. Four days later, the musician was found dead in the street. Neruda went to the wake, opened the coffin and gave his friend a kiss on the forehead. "It was an awful moment, and from it that beautiful poem for Revueltas was born," recalls Andrés Henestrosa.

The arrival of Lola Falcón and her son Poli convinced the Neruda couple to find a bigger house so they could all live together. They moved to an enormous mansion, the Quinta Rosa María, near Barranca del Muerto Station in Mixcoac.

The badger continued to claim its victims. A matchmaking Neruda asked María Izquierdo, who was wearing her badger fur, to use it to calm the agitated "Child." In the fire of their honeymoon connection, he joked, the badger fur had got tangled up on itself and died. The poet, good with nicknames, would forever refer to the painter as the "Badger Lady". When the animal ruined a Christmas for Poli Délano by biting him, they decided to send it to the zoo. Delia and Lola visited it in its confinement, and both were convinced that "the Child" recognized them when they arrived.

The enormity of the mansion's garden lent itself to the festivities. A great banquet was given in honor of the German novelist Anna Seghers; Neruda rented tables and chairs for two hundred people, and Lola had to worry about all the details of the meal. Delia dedicated herself to asking if everything was okay, and extending invitations to anyone who crossed her path.

At the big party to celebrate the baptism of Cibeles, Andrés Henestrosa's daughter, four hundred people sang, performed onstage and danced for two entire days. It became such a disturbance that the owner decided to terminate the rental contract. They had to leave, this time for an apartment at 50 Río Elba Street, steps away from the Paseo de la Reforma.

For Delia the daily scene in Santiago de Chile became repetitive. Pablo made the same jokes to annoy her and topple her friendly, steady equilibrium. Someone would always come up to tell her: "Ant, give me some *cajeta*." And she would slap him in the face for being impertinent, and leave the party. Neruda always found an innocent who didn't know the meaning of the crude Argentine word to go up to her and say it. What meant 'milk caramel' in Mexico translated to 'vulva' in Argentine Spanish.

Delia was enthusiastic about the parties to celebrate the New Year. There was something ceremonial about them; serious and important people went, and singing "The Internationale" after twelve o'clock brought them all together.

Delia retaliated against Pablo's behavior by continuing to organize the poet's work, calling attention to his lost time and vulgar manners. Putting him on track, avoiding total disorder, became her vocation.

Frequent trips seemed to balance their relationship. Their shared experiences and affection helped them to overcome the bad periods. Although the comparison with a child is absurd, Pablo was obedient in private life and had an enormous respect for Delia's opinions. Every literary step he took, every text he composed, he first consulted with her.

"This isn't good, Pablo, it starts to fall apart, it's missing a final chord."

"Then you write it."

"How can that even occur to you? You're the poet, you're a tease, go work on it a little more."

And she was right.

The outings through Mexican territory strengthened their relationship. The two shared a very fine sensibility, appreciating the landscape and admiring the tremendous changes in the countryside as it rolled past them.

Neruda had grown fanatical about snails and seashells, and he began to collect them in astronomical quantities during the three years of his stay in Mexico.

They went to Guatemala and also, for the first time, to Cuba.

In both countries, the poet gave readings and was received with applause by the cultural world.

His passion for snails was always present. In Cuba the couple was amazed by a forest filled with "polymitas", a genus of large, multicolored land snail that moved through the branches. There was no alternative; they had to take along a few samples of this fantastic species with its black shell, and its luminous concentric green, yellow and red lines. Where could they put them? The Ant's two suitcases were emptied of clothing and filled with snails. They returned holding paper bags with their clothes.

In 1942, sad news arrived to them from different places.

In Buenos Aires, Amparo Mom had died of cancer, three days before the arrival of the Alberti couple from its long exile in Argentina.

Miguel Hernández had died of tuberculosis in the infirmary of the Alicante prison, the last of the twelve prisons he had passed through during his three years in jail.

And a telegram from the Netherlands announced the death of Neruda's daughter, Malva Marina, due to the natural process of her congenital disease.

Delia was inconsolable; she had said goodbye to Amparo shortly before they left for Mexico, when she had looked to be in good health, although grieving over the abandonment of her husband Raúl González Tuñón, who had fallen hopelessly in love with Blanca Macfadzen, one of the beauties of the Santiago group.

They were frustrated by Miguel's death, thinking that maybe more could have been done, something more than the letters and messages and steps taken by important people that had resulted in nothing. Permission hadn't even been given to transfer him to a sanatorium for tuberculosis patients after the illness presented its first symptoms. He'd only been granted permission to marry his lifelong wife Josefina Manresa, the mother of his children, in a Catholic ceremony. The only option had been marriage through the Church, because in Spain, civil matrimony was not valid. Helplessness, grief and memories.

The death of his daughter prompted Neruda to begin divorce procedures with María Antonieta Hagenaar. He brought the request to the court of Tetecala, in the state of Morelos. The grounds were "unjustified desertion of the conjugal home and obligations inherent in matrimony, and incompatibility of character". A few days later the link was declared permanently dissolved, because Maruca had obviously not presented herself, and was announced to be in default.

At one o'clock in the afternoon on July 2, 1943, in the city of Tetecala in the state of Morelos, Neftalí Reyes Basoalto, which was Neruda's birth name, contracted marriage with Delia del Carril Iraeta. The two said they were divorcees; the bride dedicated herself to domestic work and was forty-five years old, while he was born in Parral and was thirty-nine years old. "On the part of the groom, the witnesses are Óscar Schnake Vergara, Chilean ambassador, and Luis Enrique Délano Díaz. For the bride, they are Wenceslao Roces Suárez, native to Oviedo, Spain, and Enrique de los Ríos Lavín from Chile," reads the certificate authenticated by the civil lawyer Jesús Castillo López, constitutional governor of the free and sovereign state of Morelos.

Despite the summer heat and the swarms of sand flies that left no one in peace, the celebratory lunch took place in the open air with songs, poetry and an enthusiasm that lasted until nightfall. Pablo gave the bride a necklace of silver cast in Oaxaca, which fit her perfectly. If she'd magically deleted fourteen years from her marriage certificate, she gave no grounds for doubt, as her appearance would make no one suspect she was on the verge of sixty years old.

In August of the same year, Neruda resigned from his consular work. He was given a farewell party in Mexico, which two thousand people attended. They then set out to return to Chile, via a long trip through the countries of the continent.

In Lima they happened to stay at the same hotel as Victoria Ocampo. Her relationship with Neruda was distant—the poet had harshly criticized the collaborators of the magazine *Sur*, particularly Pierre Drieu La Rochelle, due to his Nazi sympathies—so she was surprised when he appeared with Delia to greet her, and even gave her a present.

The President of Peru, Manuel Prado, offered his visitors the means to travel to the ruins of Machu Picchu, which had been discovered in 1911, and weren't yet the tourist site of today. The couple made a strenuous trip by mule and many journeys on foot, following the steep tracks. It took them three days to get there. "A fantastic place that reminded me of the ruins of Pompeii," remembered Delia. "You could see the remains of food and glasses of wine inside the houses. You could see the life they led... very remarkable, without a doubt."

They arrived in Chile at last on November 3, at Los Cerrillos Airport. Friends waited once again for the Neruda couple, who settled for a few days at the Carrera Hotel and then at Sylvia Thayer's apartment on 40 Vicuña Mackenna Avenue, as they waited for repairs to finish at the Lynch house. They had inquired about the residence before leaving for Mexico, and the sale was finalized by Graciela Matte with Neruda's power of attorney in February 1941.

Sylvia Thayer was the sister of Álvaro Hinojosa, a friend from the poet's youth. There was a literary gathering at her house almost every day, where it was usual to find the writer Augusto D'Halmar and the poet Ángel Cruchaga. But the way the Neruda couple settled into other people's homes had an invasive quality to it, and this was no exception.

Another guest at the house was Antonia Ramos, a young Argentine woman who had studied at the University of Chile. For her, living together with the poet and Delia was a unique experience: "They went to lunch at the house one day, and saw there was a vacant room. We're coming here, they said. They purchased a matrimonial bed and settled in. They brought trunks and more trunks full of collections. Pablo was already fat and bald. She was slim and very refined, with splendid manners; she moved her hands, her neck, her voice in a beautiful way. She was at ease, human, precise and simple. Distracted and tremendously absent-minded. Worried about beauty, but needing someone else to style it. A hairdresser came to dye her a platinum blonde, since she was going gray. I myself helped to wave her hair many times, or comb it. Whether something was missing or there, she never noticed. Pablo was too bohemian. They'd show up at two in the morning, wake everyone up and stay talking until four or five. The house transformed into an anthill of Spanish refugees and people from Mexico, you can't imagine what that was like… She lived at the rhythm of Pablo and the bohemia. They had that house completely for free, which they didn't care about in the slightest. But she was restrained, and handled with great patience and style the vulgarity of their life in common. She was elegance, he was an enfant terrible."

The new Spaniards who had arrived in Santiago were opposed by conservative groups. But it didn't take long before the effects of their presence could be seen. They stimulated a cultural life in which nothing much happened. The bohemia moved about the seedy bars, bookstores, publishing houses and cafés, especially one on Miraflores Street. There were a few rivalries with Chilean writers and artists who grudgingly accepted the intellectual superiority of the refugees. Arguments were born out of these jokes, in which differences were stamped.

One of the owners of Café Miraflores, Joaquín Berasaluce, took pride at his chefs' skill at preparing the dishes of a long list of Basque specialties. When a client simply ordered a creole *bistec a lo pobre* [poor man's steak], he couldn't hold back his fury. Sticking his head through the large window of the kitchen into the dining room, he would shout: "*Bistec a lo pobre*, what an imagination!"

The best bookstore was the Lope de Vega, named after the famous Spanish Golden Age playwright. Darío Carmona, who had been secretary to Neruda in Paris, worked there. He told this anecdote to begin his taunts.

"A client arrived, Chilean obviously, and told me: 'I want to speak with Señor Lope de Vega.' That's me, I joked. But the man insisted. 'No, no,' he said to me, 'Señor Lope de Vega had glasses.'

He was convinced that the owner, Miguel González, was Lope de Vega."

Some grew infuriated by the stories, and said to them: 'You may be very learned, you may have many monuments, but it seems that you lack toilets.'

Despite the incidents, it was at Café Miraflores, decorated with caricatures by Santiago Ontañón, the stage designer of Federico García Lorca's works, that the groups of Chileans and Spaniards worked most often. The owners of the café, along with Berasaluce, were a couple, Mina Yáñez and Pablo de la Fuente. The latter was often chased by women, despite the watchful and jealous gaze of his wife. At the café the group of poets and writers grew to incorporate architects, musicians and painters: Camilo Mori and Maruja Vargas, Antonio Aparicio and Carmen "Gigy" López; Germán Rodríguez Arias, the architect who had drawn up the designs to make Neruda's imaginative visions for his homes concrete; Jaime Valle Inclán, the painter Arturo Lorenzo, Elena Gómez de la Serna, Inés Puyó and José Ricardo Morales; Santiago Ontañón, married to Nana Bell, the daughter of Graciela Matte; Arturo Soria, founder of the publisher Cruz del Sur; and, of course, the group most intimate with Neruda, the Falcón sisters, Diego Muñoz, Acario Cotapos and Tomás Lago.

The Spaniards changed the city. They talked loudly, smoked a lot and introduced a liveliness previously unknown in Santiago. But these transformations didn't immediately influence the official world of the country, which continued to burrow into a conservatism almost impermeable to change or cultural modernization.

CHAPTER 10

1944–1955

According to those who knew him, Neruda wasn't a typical Don Juan. He didn't chase women; they chased him. Nor was he a typical seducer. He was no great lover, and didn't have an especially attractive physique. He simply made his conquests from his position as a poet, through his leadership and the appearance of power that was part of his personality. His indirect, sinuous style, bolstered by his own conviction of his worth, operated as a powerful stimulant. The appeal of a clandestine act played a part in his varied and fleeting relationships. It also helped that there were many men and women prepared to watch his back. "The women hovered around Pablo like flies," said Elena Caffarena.

Delia wasn't a possessive or jealous woman. She knew her own importance as the wife of the poet. Her exaggerated admiration for Neruda led to her unconditional loyalty—loyalty toward his work, his politics and his health. She took excessive precautions. To fight Pablo's corpulence, she bought small weights to measure out the exact quantities of foods he should eat. She took precautions with herself, too. She'd just submitted to a treatment at the Clínica Santa María to help her stop smoking, as her hoarse voice irritated her. During meals she followed strict rules, like chewing meat at least seventy times, eating slowly and avoiding mixtures that she'd heard were fatal. She was an expert in proteins, fats, carbohydrates, glucoses and vitamins. These subjects interested her, and she gave classes on them.

"Pablo, only one spoonful of gourd jelly."

"Ant, I'll eat as much gourd jelly as I want, until I myself turn into a gourd."

The laughter put an end to the matter. Delia's discipline didn't result in much. But she kept trying.

The other area where she exercised control was in politics. Whenever the Communist Party requested the poet's presence, there they were, giving lyrical speeches about ideology, going on tours, attending demonstrations, and traveling to Concepción and Temuco or the north, wherever the Party liked.

These were years of feverish movement. They received many visits at "Michoacán" as they'd named the house on Lynch Street, in memory of the Mexican years. Paul Valéry and Miguel Ángel Asturias were received with their characteristic parties. So were María Teresa León and Rafael Alberti, who lived in Argentina. A visit from the Cuban poet Nicolás Guillén enjoyed some of the most intense festivities. In gratitude, Guillén wrote a poem read at the goodbye meal, later published in the Sunday supplement of the newspaper *El Siglo* in 1947.

This Pablo Neruda, great Chil-
a son and father from frigid Temu-
is our glory and our pri-

not in Chile but in all Ame-
a train of blood runs through his vei-
and he launches his verse which is shar-
made of a strange metal, a metal which is har-
that the people considers its ow-
greedy Pablo keeps a great trea-
that all of us consider ou-
and is not coal or copper or saltpet-
this treasure dreamed of by Pa-
they name, or they call or ca-
the Ant, the little Ant, the A-

This political effervescence and social life gave the couple a special feeling of closeness, a mutual understanding that didn't involve fits of passion, but rather solidified their matrimony through shared projects.

Diego Muñoz, now separated from Regina Falcón, came to live in the Lynch house with his current partner, Inés Valenzuela. Despite an enormous age different—Inés was only eighteen years old—she got along perfectly with Delia, who was older than her mother. For Delia, such differences didn't exist.

The Ant had ordered a studio built in the garden, where in secret and very occasionally she made paintings using acrylic paint, a technique she'd learned in classes with the Uruguayan painter Verdesio in Mexico. Only Diego Muñoz, who had also taken painting classes and was interested in the subject, was allowed to come into the studio to make comments on these works. Delia struggled with drawing and color, with interruptions and limited time.

At Michoacán the party continued. At the nearby delicatessen they racked up astronomical sums. One can even find a receipt for a lamb, purchased by a guest as a gift. Delia made a daily visit to the kitchen, which was rather unnecessary since she got up so late. "What have you thought about making for today's lunch?" The cook explained to her what he was preparing, and invariably she'd say: "That sounds very good to me." Having done so, she felt she'd more than fulfilled her role as head of the household. So many people came for lunch that meals had to emerge out of improvisations of which she was completely unaware, immersed as she was in more abstract conversations.

"Don't you think, darling, that Pablo and Diego are both slow in the head? They're absolutely slow in the head," said Delia to Inés, half appalled and half amused, as they stood at the gates of the Embassy of Czechoslovakia, where they'd been invited for dinner. They needed to arrive at nine o'clock sharp. The two men had spoken all day long about the rigorous punctuality of diplomats, and the importance of showing up at exactly nine o'clock. It was raining torrents in Santiago, and on Lynch Street the water flowed like a river. Neruda and Diego Muñoz leisurely crossed the street to the car where their wives were waiting, dressed elegantly for the reception. At the moment that the Ambassador and his wife came out to receive them, the deafening noise of an alarm clock came from the poet's coat: "We made it, we arrived on time, Diego!" And Delia to Inés: "They act like they're slow in the head, darling."

Marvelous news arrived from Argentina. At last they'd been able to sell the building on Garay Street. The money provided an excellent monthly income. Elena Caffarena and Jorge Jiles, their lawyers, decided on a safe investment. Among friends the news was celebrated. Pablo's economic problems were over. The poet, who was extremely sensitive to any personal matter that might give rise to gossip, was attentive to the envy that his prominent position created. He saw bad intentions at every step, and cut them off with acidic replies to anyone who dared make a joke. Nothing disturbed him more than to be the subject of a comment that affected him.

With part of this money, two and a half million pesos, Delia became the owner of the Lynch house, paying one hundred and ninety-six thousand pesos, the same amount as Pablo owed to the Public Employees' Fund.

Almost all the rest of the Ant's money ended in disaster. A friend of Neruda's, thought to have a good business in Valparaíso, offered to manage the capital, promising a juicy income. For a few months everything worked perfectly, but later it was discovered that the man had declared bankruptcy, and some time after this he died in a car accident. There was nobody to answer for anything.

The Party named Neruda as its candidate for Senator in the provinces of Tarapacá and Antofagasta. He was chosen from a list of communists and radicals that included Elías Lafertte and Gabriel González Videla. The Popular Front continued to win followers. After the death of President Aguirre Cerda, Juan Antonio Ríos replaced him, and when he died after finishing his term of office, González Videla was presented as candidate. Neruda was named his Head of Publicity, and worked hard on the campaign that carried him to the presidency.

But the banners being hoisted in the world had changed. After the Allied victory and the defeat of fascism, a new age had begun. The time when Nelson Rockefeller had traveled through Latin America to meet with communist comrades and bring them to work on anti-fascist programs at the State Department in Washington was over. The United States was in a full-on battle against its old allies, Stalin and Soviet communism.

The new government led by Gabriel González Videla began under these conditions. The cabinet was made up of military figures and independents. But as everyone knows, in politics, independence is a virtue exclusive to the right.

Chilean communists reacted against this turn. They encouraged the most important labor unions to strike at the coal mines of Lota in the south of the country, and mobilized all the groups of workers that had closed ranks with the Party. The social discontent seemed unstoppable.

Then came the Law for the Defense of Democracy, the "Law Maldita" [Damned Law] as it was referred to later. The government responded to communist agitation with raids, persecutions, prisons and concentration camps. This didn't only affect the militants. Sympathizers and foreigners, like many of the Spaniards who had arrived on the *Winnipeg*, were also targeted. Communism moved underground.

Neruda's statements to a Venezuelan newspaper, with their direct and forceful criticisms of González Videla, and his speeches in the Senate on the same lines, did him in. They were followed by political trial, impeachment from the Senate, confirmation by the Supreme Court and a detention order.

While the Senate opened the session that was certain to result in a vote against him, Pablo and Delia decided to leave for Mendoza. But at the border in Los Andes, customs officials discovered a contradiction between the poet's identity card and his passport. One said Pablo Neruda, and the other Neftalí Reyes. They didn't let him pass.

Pablo and Delia made the return journey while mulling over whose house they could take refuge in. The people in the party were all being watched. They decided on a Chilean engineer, a man who didn't appear in public but whom they trusted, a member of their protective staff: José Saitúa Pedemonte, married to a Spanish refugee, Gloria Nistal. Neither Neruda nor Delia knew the couple in person.

They reached their house on Los Leones Street at three in the morning. In his memoirs, Gabriel González Videla plays down this moment: "[W]e knew where he was, what he was doing, but I didn't want to give him the pleasure of being a hero [...] The situation gave rise to one of the most grotesque comedies, the one about the persecuted poet, the poet in chains."

If Neruda's fame previously hadn't reached beyond a select group interested in poetry, then his photos in the newspapers and the rewards for his capture, announced in prominent advertisements, now made him known throughout the country.

For an entire year, Delia and Pablo had to remain hidden, changing their addresses, adjusting to a permanent confinement.

The Saitúa house didn't seem safe, as there were maids who could inform against them. During the first days a persistent nervousness reigned, and the surprise of suddenly being prevented from carrying out even the slightest activity made daily life feel like a trainwreck. Any routine was blocked by the threat of persecution.

The Party implemented a complex plan to help. They moved Pablo and Delia to an unoccupied sixth-floor apartment belonging to Víctor Pey on Vicuña Mackenna Street, at the corner of Eulogia Sánchez, which seemed like a more secure location. Pey had arrived on the *Winnipeg*. He was grateful to the Neruda couple, and wanted to give them a hand in return. He looked after them, bringing them food every day, carrying out errands and fulfilling requests. Police novels from the Seventh Circle collection for Neruda. Whisky and good food from the Eastern Establishments grocery store, near the apartment. And for the Ant, jars of a special cream from Petrizzio Pharmacy which she smeared on her face, dyes for her graying hair, and paper and charcoal pencils for drawing.

The poet's anguish increased; sometimes he dared go up to the terrace of the building at night with Víctor Pey. At least there he could breathe calmly and admire the sky. Once, they were seen by the concierge. To avoid trouble, they called him after breaking a water tap in the bathroom so that he could repair it. This gave him a chance to see that there was nobody else there, besides the owner of the house. While the man was working, Delia and Pablo stayed shut away in a closet for over half an hour.

The couple's life, which had been stabilized by their working habits and the presence of so many people around them, began to deteriorate with this isolation, this forced co-existence, this uncertainty about their condition.

After a month they tried an unsuccessful weekend trip to Valparaíso. When they came back, they insisted on staying in houses that weren't vacant.

Aída Figueroa and Sergio Insunza were lawyers who had just married, members of the Party who lived in an apartment facing the Parque Forestal. They had recently hosted other people who had gone underground, coal union leaders who had fled from Lota owing to persecution. So it wasn't strange for them to receive a request to host two people.

Even so, when they opened the door and faced the famous poet and his wife, their surprise was tremendous.

The Ant immediately broke the ice: "What a beautiful living room, and you have a piano, how marvelous, what delightful furniture, how lovely, and what an incredible view of the park. What woman could be more charming than you, what little baby more precious…" Her enthusiasm knew no bounds.

When Aída offered to make special arrangements and give them their own bedroom, Delia emphatically refused: "By no means, we'll sleep like teaspoons in this little bed."

They lived there for almost two months. The rhythm of the house changed completely. They took over the living room, where Pablo worked. Delia lingered for ages in her bedroom, getting dressed and making herself up to excess, with white lead and rouge on her face, deep black shadows on her eyes and bright red lip pencil. She spent hours on her hair, which was her obsession, curling it with pieces of paper that covered her entire head and making sure that it was dyed, while asking for help with everything.

Neruda worked in the mornings on the *Canto General*, settling into the living room with a portable typewriter. Afterward the Ant gathered the pages and began the work of "pointing out the errors every writer commits". Taking notes on the original, she drew attention to dissonances and redundancies. The work needed a great deal of historical and geographical information, and it was Aída who went to the National Library to get hold of the material.

The closeness of the Central Market and the good cook at the house inspired the poet's imagination. He ordered ducks, conger eels and shellfish for the finest moment of the day, lunch, which ended in a long siesta.

If life seemed to smile on the Neruda couple in that place, where the view of the park gave them an impression of freedom, their young married hosts lived through a period of exhaustion. In addition to the rhythm of the visitors, with their whims and requests and long nocturnal conversations, they had the obligations of jobs with fixed schedules, a household to run and the endless challenges of family life.

Complicating matters for the poet, the government brought María Antonieta Hagenaar from the Netherlands, supporting her with judicial assistance to initiate claims of bigamy and alimony against Neruda. The matter ended with a monetary agreement: Maruca received three hundred thousand pesos in exchange for a signature agreeing to complete settlement. From underground, Neruda was represented by the lawyer Fernando Silva Yocham.

The final hideaway was the house of Simón Telerman on 777 Miguel Claro Street, where they remained for over a month. But Jorge Bellet and Víctor Pey had already agreed on a plan to leave through the south for Argentina, with the approval of the Party.

This year of moving from one place to another, with some happy moments and many disagreeable ones, left a dent in the marriage. When Delia realized she wasn't included in the plans for escape, because it was a difficult and dangerous operation that included crossing the mountain range—not easy even for one person, and complicated further by a couple—she screamed blue murder. Naturally, the one who would struggle with the escape was Pablo, since he didn't ride a horse and didn't have her resilience; Delia could do it flawlessly. But her arguments were no use. According to some, it was Pablo who was opposed to her coming on the trip, but he needed other people to confront her about it.

Pablo and the Ant said goodbye to one another at the house of Graciela Matte, on 66 Monseñor Cabrera Street. From there he left for the south, to Graneros, in the car of Doctor Raúl Bulnes, a friend and neighbor from Isla Negra as well as a form of protection, since he'd been a medic for the Border Guards. Víctor Pey was waiting for him in a red Chevrolet provided by another friend, Manuel Solimano. Pey and Bulnes returned to Santiago, while Neruda and Jorge Bellet headed south. The operation worked perfectly.

The deprivations of that year ended with a thunderous reception in Paris, at the World Congress of the Defenders of the Peace. At the same time, the government in Chile announced that in only a few hours Neruda would be arrested.

Delia stayed for a few days at Graciela Matte's house, and then moved to Víctor Pey's mother's house. She waited day after day for some communication, any news, in a state of troubled spirits. After two months, she traveled to Poland to meet with Neruda.

Given the political circumstances of the Cold War, the poet was given a seat of honor within the party, which elevated him to the status of a global figure. Neruda came to be an indispensable character at world congresses for culture and peace backed by the Soviet Union. His work began to be translated and published in Eastern countries.

They spent the rest of the year making trips to the Soviet Union, Romania and Hungary.

In the Soviet Union they were received by Stalin himself, who gave Delia a magnificent astrakhan coat with a red silk lining, very light despite its appearance. They met other important writers and artists. Delia felt every distinction given to Pablo as her own, like his appointment as council member for the Lenin Peace Prize.

In Romania she made a discovery that dazzled her: the medical advances of Doctor Ana Aslan for health and rejuvenation. She underwent all the treatments with mud and vitamin-supplemented medicines that had made the doctor famous. Delia was already sixty-five years old, and by her side was a man who was twenty years younger. The years had left their mark, and she knew it. She threw herself into the study of all of Ana Aslan's theories, fulfilling to the letter her recommendations about eating vegetables and stocking up generously on her creams and concoctions.

After returning to Paris, they went on a trip to Mexico for the Latin American Congress of Supporters of the Peace, accompanied by Paul Éluard and his new wife, Dominique, an active communist militant. Dominique and Delia got along immediately.

Gabriela Mistral was also in Mexico. She'd settled in Veracruz, and the Neruda couple visited her. A North American woman of status named Doris Dana, thirty years younger than Mistral, was living with her and doing much to cheer up the poet after her dismissal from *El Mercurio*, the Chilean newspaper where she'd worked.

The trip to Mexico lasted longer than planned. Neruda suffered from grave thrombophlebitis. He stayed in bed without moving for two months and underwent a complicated treatment with anticoagulants. It wasn't unusual for the Neruda couple to receive friends in their room, but this time it was an imposition. And, as always, friends were not lacking.

After an immense amount of work, Neruda finished editing *Canto General*. Siqueiros and Diego Rivera contributed paintings for the covers. With its large format and its red and black letters, the publication was reminiscent of old missals. Near the end of the book, it contained a poem for Delia:

> *I want to be swept*
> *downward by the rains that the wild*
> *sea wind combats and fragments,*
> *then flow through subterranean channels, go on*
> *toward the deep springtime being reborn.*
> *Open beside me the hollow of the one I love, and one day*
> *may she accompany me again in the earth.*

(from "Disposiciones" ["Dispositions"] in *Canto General*)

166

Galope lento (Paz para los hombres) [Slow Gallop (Peace for Mankind)],
engraving made by Delia in Paris, 1959.

The edition was five hundred copies, and three hundred were made for subscribers in a special large format on Malinche paper, signed by the author and two painters in a public presentation. Among the subscribers, there were friends from every country, including Adelina del Carril Güiraldes, Adolfo Aráoz Alfaro and Sara Tormú de Rojas Paz in Argentina, and Paul Éluard, Pablo Picasso and Fernand Léger in France.

During Neruda's illness a woman appeared who was prepared to take care of him and look after the house. This was Matilde Urrutia, a Chilean who was spending a season in Mexico. They had met at one of his readings. In reality, she had waited for him after a reading ended, in order to speak with him. Neruda didn't remember their previous encounter in Chile, when she had been a student of Blanca Hauser's, but the attraction born from those forgotten days now reemerged with full strength.

After the poet recovered, Matilde accompanied them on a trip to Guatemala, and said goodbye to them when they went to Europe.

But they wouldn't be separated for long. Neruda carried out a complicated operation to distract Delia and recover Matilde, which began in Berlin during another conference. Previously he'd invited his lover to Paris. In Germany he arranged for her to be hired as a singer at the Third World Youth Festival, another branch of the Party's cultural programming.

On subsequent trips, Matilde would always make a surprise appearance, even during a visit to the Soviet Union when the Trans-Siberian train brought them to the Mongolian People's Republic. When the coincidence started to become too great, she appeared as the supposed lover and companion of Nicolás Guillén, so she could travel with them. Neruda moved mountains and used accomplices to achieve his end.

He didn't always manage it. On a series of trips through Italy, Hungary and Romania, which afterward brought them to India and China, Matilde had to be left out. A chance meeting so far away was too implausible.

Matilde complained and made veiled threats of abandonment. The poet, enraptured and indecisive, had to make conclusive plans.

Perhaps Delia suspected. But there was no chance of Neruda giving up this affair. The situation was unsustainable

He put an end to the never-ending trips by dedicating himself to writing. His legs—which he had to keep bandaged—also demanded rest. He settled in with Delia in Capri. Gabriela Mistral, who had come back from Mexico to live in Naples, found them a perfect place to live. Once he was settled, Pablo convinced Delia to return to Chile, to finally end her exile and resolve the judicial cases against her.

Some observers, more concerned with legend than reality, tell of a possible suicide attempt by Delia at that house, but there is no evidence of anything like this, and what happened later leaves no room to suspect it.

It's possible that she could sense a strange distance in Pablo's attitude, but in her favor she had that distraction, that ability to be dazzled by a detail that served as a perfect mechanism for evasion.

Before leaving for Buenos Aires in January 1952, she wrote this suggestive and moving letter to Gabriela Mistral:

> My Dearest, don't take this as sentimentalism, romanticism, sad thoughts or strange forebodings. I'm leaving tomorrow. I know that the same risks might be run in the streets of a city or the four walls of a bedroom if fate *s'en mêle*, but with Pablo we've always talked, every time that we travel, about each of us making a will. We've never made this project into a reality, and I can't do so now, since I know there are formal procedures I

don't understand, which can be tricky in a foreign country. But I'd like to leave a record before Lucila Godoy, consul of Chile and my dear admired friend Gabriela Mistral, that everything I possess as Delia del Carril de Reyes in Chile, or as Delia del Carril in Argentina, will go through my will by inalienable right to Pablo Neruda. I know that this declaration in a letter has no more value than what you give to it with your immense prestige, but it would be decisive should the matter arise. I'm not afraid of any wrong actions on the part of my family, but it isn't for nothing that the two of us have always thought of making a will. As soon as I get to Buenos Aires, I will legalize this ideal. Sending you much love Gabriela… Give my love to Pablo, too. Kisses to Doris. Delia del Carril de Reyes.

In Buenos Aires she stayed for a while at the apartment on Las Heras Street, which belonged to the Alberti couple. Afterward, she moved to the house of her sister-in-law María Elena Videla Dorna, to be with her niece Teresa and her nephew Conrado, the sons of her favorite brother Víctor who had died four years earlier, and to whom she hadn't been able to say goodbye. The children were delighted by this special aunt, so different from the rest of the family, who treated them as grown-ups, worried over their interests, had the word "careful!" on the tip of her tongue whenever they caused a commotion that she thought seemed dangerous or a bad word escaped their lips, and talked with them about the injustices of the world and the wonders of socialism.

The niece and nephew gave her the nickname "Red Nun". She paid attention to the world and knew an entire Buenos Aires that they'd never suspected. Artists, poets and politicians called on her and she went out with them for the entire day.

"Back of your head, Aunt Delia," Teresita would say to her when she saw her going out in a rush, all dressed up, but with hair flat and messy on the back of her neck. And Delia would laugh and ask for help, as always.

She returned to Chile, to the Lynch house which had been left in the hands of her sister-in-law Laurita Reyes. Letters from Pablo from Capri were waiting for her, many letters that were affectionate and false. "My Ant: here is your lonely grasshopper in the cold sun of Capri..." "...a thousand kisses from Pablo..." She ran errands, delivering messages to their friends, asking them to help lift the prohibition on his return, and arranging the move of his thousand possessions. He sent telegrams that she didn't understand. "Dispatch necessary. Pablo." Her friend Lucía Amion de Vadell easily clarified: he needed money.

Of course Pablo wasn't alone. Matilde had arrived after Delia's departure, and for the first time they were living without fear of surprises.

Facing popular discontent, the government of González Videla was coming to its end. The turn toward the right had been definitive. The powerful Radical Party, which had found a platform in the middle class by defining itself as secular, socialist and democratic, was splitting apart.

The Senate had requested amnesty for Neruda, as had Gabriela Mistral and other figures. The government limited itself to ambiguous declarations. But with these maneuvers, it cleared the stage for his return, which occurred in August with enough fanfare to force González Videla to desist from any action.

In the meantime Delia presided over a kind of regency, surrounded by friends in the Michoacán house, waiting for Pablo's return with Graciela Matte, Delia Solimano, the wife of Tomás Lago at the time, and their close collaborators.

When Pablo returned, all doubts seemed to dissolve. He and the Ant formed a solid political and social institution. They surrounded themselves with sympathizers and Party activists, and many writers, artists and distinguished figures in Santiago gathered around them.

Neruda dedicated himself industriously to the presidential campaign of Salvador Allende. He had emerged from an agreement between the parties on the left, which were greatly weakened by the persecution of the Government and from systematic and belligerent propaganda on the world stage.

Allende's candidacy didn't end in a presidential salute to the flag. The right, too, was defeated in elections. The one chosen as leader was Carlos Ibáñez del Campo, the "General of Hope". Ibáñez, who had been sent packing after his previous dictatorial government, returned in glory with a populist program and an ideology similar to that of his Argentine neighbor, Juan Domingo Perón. He had his Evita too—not his wife, but a passionate and zealous supporter, María de la Cruz, a woman who was eloquently bold and convincing, qualities the General lacked. "Bring Ibáñez to power, bring the broom to sweep" was the domestic battle cry that convinced the public to vote for him, certain that he would be able to destroy the enclaves of power that protected a small minority.

Culture was once again the weapon wielded by the Communist Party. Neruda, with the experience of his exile, began to create institutions and organize international meetings the likes of which had never been seen before in Chile.

Politicians joined the groups that came to Lynch. Delia led meetings and shared her opinions with stylish ease. The Eye of Molotov was back in action.

The return of Neruda was also the return of Matilde. They devised new tactics and schemes, more dangerous now that they were in Chile.

The first to raise the alarm was María, the wife of César Godoy Urrutia, a friend of the Neruda couple, a militant in the party and a personal witness to the advances of Matilde in Mexico. María had a strong voice and a harsh tongue. She was the only one to identify Matilde for what she was, and she made sure that everyone heard her.

On October 27, 1952, Delia and Pablo had a car accident near their house. He suffered a wound to his right arm. It was put in a cast and he was sent home. Delia remained unconscious for hours, staying for two days under observation at the public assistance center in Ñuñoa.

The news was transmitted over the radio. Many visitors appeared to check on the accident victims.

Matilde's concern for Pablo made them commit their first mistake. She settled into Lynch to look after him until Delia's arrival.

At the end of the year, the Neruda couple set off on another trip to Moscow to participate in the Second Congress of Writers. Volodia Teitelboim accompanied them. They settled into the luxurious Metropol Hotel in large, splendid apartments, where they received intellectuals and politicians and organized the same parties that Pablo seemed to repeat wherever he was.

Hit with a nasty flu and a high fever, he decided to return to Chile at all costs. Delia didn't understand this madness, this idea of leaving so quickly and out of the blue, sick as he was. Volodia couldn't betray his friend by answering Delia's questions. She imagined that he knew something more.

The reason was clear. Matilde couldn't bear the idea of a trip without her and had sent him an ultimatum, threatening to leave for a northern country forever if he wasn't with her by the end of the year.

The country was Mexico, and it meant that she'd decided to return to an old lover, a powerful man who was waiting for her.

Matilde Urrutia's life had been difficult. Born in poverty in Chillán, she left for Santiago and worked at Post Office Two in the Barrio Sur neighborhood of Santiago. She began singing lessons with Blanca Hauser, with the intention of embarking on a singing career, but she wasn't cut out for it. She completed a few tours through Latin America that didn't result in anything greater. Her sentimental life hadn't found a definite path, either. Although later she was known to have had distinguished lovers, her relationship with the poet was the most important thing in her life up to that point. She was thirty-four years old when they met. It was understandable that she'd do the unspeakable to assure herself a place.

Neruda tried to keep things in a confused balance and avoid any consequences. His fame both eased and complicated the task.

Organizing and attending congresses, working for the Party, and a heap of other obligations were good excuses to stay away from Lynch. Poems and ardent letters buoyed Matilde's enthusiasm when he couldn't be there.

The publication of *Los versos del capitán* [The Captain's Verses] by an anonymous author, following their stay in Capri, raised suspicions. Those who knew the truth had perhaps not been very discreet, and those in the know claimed to recognize his hand in the poetry, although it could also have been his influence on someone unknown.

"Everybody says the book is yours," Delia said to him.

In Brazil, an expert, the Uruguayan teacher Jesualdo Sosa, repeatedly insisted to them that it was Neruda's work. Volodia Teitelboim, eyewitness to the episode, remembers Delia's confusion and the poet's anger as he tried to silence the meddler.

THE ANT

They'd gone to Brazil for a Congress of Culture organized by Jorge Amado and funded by the Party, similar to the one that had taken place months before in Santiago de Chile. The Latin American intellectuals in attendance became friends and formed an influential bloc, just as the Europeans had done in previous decades. The Soviet Union supported and protected them, even when their own governments were suspicious of these activities.

Among friends, the evidence of Neruda's new relationship was subjected to all kinds of commentaries. In a game of who knows most, they went about accumulating precedents. The hidden presence of Matilde at the poet's readings was noted with elbow nudges. The construction of a house on the hillside of San Cristóbal was also part of the speculations. The painter Camilo Mori and Maruja Vargas saw the new construction from the window of their house, but when they met Pablo nearby in the street, he always claimed he was there for mysterious Party meetings.

María de Godoy Urrutia continued to smear Matilde's reputation. Nobody could believe that the Ant would remain in limbo. Neruda was constantly aware of what was being said. His greatest worry was that things might come to the ears of the people in the Party. He feared communist morals, as delicate as Catholic ones.

In addition, there were other enemies whose sole desire was a scandal of these proportions. This is why Neruda was upset by the words of the El Mercurio literary critic Hernán Díaz Arrieta, "Alone", who with a sharp quill wrote in his recently published Historia personal de la literatura chilena [Personal History of Chilean Literature]: "The rise of Pablo Neruda, in this century of great spectacles, is one of the most impressive and, for those who knew him when he was 'green', rather astonishing…"

A great distraction would be needed to avoid the inevitable. He convinced Delia to travel to Paris and take responsibility for the deluxe edition of *Canto General*. He asked her to revise it and pay special attention to the translation; he insisted that her work was essential because no one knew the poems like her, and she had to convince Fernand Léger to illustrate the book.

Delia went to work, and became newly interested in the mysteries of engraving as Léger prepared art for this edition. She revised the translation and visited the printer at 33 Rue Saint-André-des-Arts, where she was moved once more by the words dedicated to her.

Ouvre près de moi la tombe de celle que j'aime, et qu'un jour
elle m'acompagne un fois encore dans la terre.
[*Open beside me the hollow of the one I love, and one day*
may she accompany me again in the earth.]

She didn't wait for the book to come out. She felt that something wasn't right, and she wanted to return to Chile as soon as possible. The first days of March she boarded the *Andes* ship in Cherbourg toward Buenos Aires.

During this period, maybe she confessed her problems to her sister Adelina, or something in her attitude reflected these worries. The fact is that Adelina promised to visit her in Chile soon.

After inviting many friends for Pablo's fiftieth birthday party, which would be celebrated in July, she returned to Santiago in the company of her nephew Conrado, who had to leave Buenos Aires because of financial worries. His company seemed necessary to her at that moment.

Pablo had spent almost the entire time of her absence at Isla Negra, and had prepared two books that he insisted reach the printer before his birthday. These were *Las uvas y el viento* [The Grapes and the Wind], poems about exile and his trips through so many countries, and *Odas elementales* [Elemental Odes], with which he especially wanted to celebrate.

Over the course of several nights, friends gathered to listen to the new poems. One evening is remembered as especially moving. The poet began to read:

My love, as if one day
you died
and I dug
and dug
night and day
in your grave
and put you together again,
raised your breasts from the dust,
the mouth I adored from its ashes,
reconstructed
your arms and your legs and your eyes,
your hair of twisted metal,
and gave you life
with the love that loves you,
made you walk anew,
throb once more against my waist,
that, my love, is the way
they rebuilt Warsaw.

(from "Regresó la sirena" [Return of the Mermaid]
in *The Grapes and the Wind*)

They looked at Delia, and she was crying. Nobody made a sound. This was an unmistakable reference to the moments that Pablo was living through.

When Delia returned, she had one of those episodes of spring cleaning that came upon her now and then. This time, maybe, it was to trace what had happened in her absence. She set the maids to ordering the shelves, the pantry, the wine cellars. She found too many hidden bottles of whisky and champagne, proof that there had been parties. In itself this wasn't strange, but their concealment suggested something suspicious.

The Lynch house prepared for Neruda's big birthday bash. Delia made long guest lists and phone calls to confirm the attendance of writers and friends from all over the world. To celebrate, Neruda had decided to donate his library to the University of Chile, along with his collection of snails.

To help sort and classify this gift, the University sent Chita Chaigneau and Marta Amunátegui to the house. They caught a glimpse of not only the preparations for the festivities, but also the domestic intimacies.

The arrival of Adelina del Carril and María Elena Videla Dorna, Delia's sister-in-law, highlighted the tension between Delia and Pablo.

Adelina decided to stay with Marta Amunátegui—who was almost a part of the family, since she was now engaged to Conrado—in order to avoid Neruda. She was very conscious of what her sister was experiencing, and in that house she could rant as much as she liked against the poet and about everything Delia had given up for the relationship, including her possessions. She was too passionate to remain silent.

The birthday celebrations delayed the end. Guests from abroad—Oliverio Girondo and Norah Lange, María Rosa Oliver, Miguel Ángel Asturias, Jorge Guillén and many more—began the week of festivities with a big meal at La Bahía restaurant, which belonged to Neruda's friend Arcadio Vadell. They followed this with readings, conferences and meetings. A disorganized meal at Lynch, where the owner insisted on a main meal of beans with spicy pork sausage, brought the commemorations to a close.

Neruda, for whom the siesta had always been a sacred rite, was in the habit of lunching at home and going out immediately afterward, despite the suspicions of the Ant. He spent his siestas and afternoons with Matilde, who was settled into an apartment on Providencia Avenue, lent to her by her supporters, Armando Carvajal and Blanca Hauser. There, a chosen few shared in the poet's double life.

Delia had already received a shock. The gardener, fired by Neruda after he was accused of stealing bottles of fine wine, told her without mincing his words: "I am a communist, Madame, and we communists do not accept these things."

She silenced him, but she'd already heard enough. The man had witnessed Matilde's presence at Lynch when the car crash had kept Delia at the public assistance center.

Neruda went too far now. He brought Matilde to Isla Negra for long periods, where she acted as lady of the house. Fed up with the poor treatment she was receiving, and aware of Delia's concern for her maids, the caretaker of the house traveled to Santiago and revealed the entire situation to the Ant.

Friends remember the Ant's emotional disastrous state at the time. Nervous, unbalanced, more distracted than ever, she exaggerated the colors of her wardrobe, wore outlandish hats and painted herself with strident make-up. Without a gaze of affection, she cut a severe figure.

Now there were very few who didn't know. Inés Valenzuela and Diego Muñoz confronted their friend.

"That's what they're going around saying."

Neruda denied everything, and called the Ant so he could tell her what he'd heard.

"They say I have a lover, and that it's Matilde Urrutia."

"And who is Matilde Urrutia?"

"But you know her, Ant, she's the woman who ironed your blouses in Mexico."

Neruda denied absolutely everything.

Nobody knows what tacit agreements, what promises, what compromises the two negotiated, but several months passed without anything being resolved. Fear, indecision, twenty years together and an uncertain future must have made it seem reasonable to prefer a waiting period, a postponement.

Delia took some drawing classes at a workshop led by Nemesio Antúnez, who had just arrived in Chile. Pablo often went to pick her up in the afternoons on Guardia Vieja Street. The painter had stayed with them in Mexico, sleeping in a big closet connected to Delia and Pablo's bedroom. During the time living together, they'd become very good friends.

Neruda moved with hesitation between Delia's attentive mistrust and Matilde's intimidations and demands for security. The construction of the new house made Matilde happy, but the expenses were too great for the poet. With his ambiguous way of giving his opinion through the words of someone else, he told her that friends believed it was turning out to be rather expensive for him. Matilde unleashed her fury, and Tomás Lago, the one who had supposedly given this opinion, moved to the top of the blacklist of her enemies.

The situation rattled Delia's natural composure. Alert and jealous, she worried about schedules and encouraged Pablo to spend enormous amounts of time writing, something she could control. Her anxiety went further, and she began to rifle through the pockets of his clothes.

At last she found the irrefutable proof, a letter Neruda had carelessly left in a jacket. In it, Matilde told him she was pregnant. (She would lose the child after two months.)

As a disciplined communist, Delia gave an account of her situation to the General Leadership. Her decision to separate from him was final.

Neruda insisted that she would always be his wife, that Matilde was prepared to occupy a secondary role.

Their conversations in front of Galo González, the General Secretary of the Party, were dramatic. The two cried, but the Ant didn't agree to the proposal, which seemed to her unacceptable.

"This isn't a bourgeois marriage, Pablo. If there's no love, there's no marriage."

The meetings continued. They took the time to think, and didn't rush.

Neruda tried to convince Delia through her girlfriends. "Matilde's done nothing more than what Delia did in Madrid when I was with Maruca; she got into my bed. How can she not understand? What's happening is that the old crones surrounding her are giving bad advice."

Delia called Nemesio Antúnez, who went urgently to her house. He found her curled up in a ball, crying on a sofa in her bedroom like a girl who'd been left by her first boyfriend.

Their last meeting was at the end of the summer of 1955 at the Lynch house, in the back of the garden by the theater they'd built in memory of García Lorca. It had seen so many performances in recent years, before this drama.

Galo González was there. So were Inés Valenzuela and Diego Muñoz, just like almost every morning. They intended to leave when the General Secretary showed up, but the couple asked them to stay.

They waited outside as the conversation went on for hours. At last Delia came and asked Inés to accompany her to her bedroom. She'd decided to leave.

"I can't accept what Pablo is proposing. Would you accept something like that?"

Inés Valenzuela didn't dare tell her what she thought. If she was seventy years old like the Ant, no doubt her choice would be different.

Delia didn't consider age to be relevant. But maybe the difference that had always seemed to be a disadvantage was precisely what enabled her dignity to prevail over the deep sadness of those days.

She settled into the home of her friend Graciela Matte. Volodia Teitelboim arrived with a letter from Pablo for the Ant, three handwritten pages. From this reply we can conclude that Delia had written a harsh, distressed letter to the poet, but it has never been found.

February 20, 1955

My dear darling Ant:

Your last letter is offensive and it's hard not to be so given our circumstances, but I won't go into the details you suggest. My admiration for you is intact, and in this case I agree we shouldn't continue to hurt each other. For my part, I've offered you all the solutions that can humanly occur to me. If you don't accept them, at least don't insult them. Nothing can erase how much you've done in our marriage, nor your words of encouragement. For my part I've done as much as I can. If you've made friendships everywhere on your own, if you're loved with tenderness by so many people, it's due to your intelligent and charming personality, but also because of the number of opportunities I've given you to meet these people and visit these countries.

As for the trips you made alone, you're wrong.

You're wrong to blame Homero (Arce, Neruda's secretary) or to speak about partners in crime.

I believe I've proceeded with all the delicacy only you deserve. Why should I say things you won't accept, as your attitude demonstrates. You say these were stabs in the back. If this were so, then the history of human life, all of life with its unavoidable changes, would be only a history of stabs in the back.

Your part in my life is established whatever you do, and if I've made a mistake or been unjust, forgive me as you know how. As for me, I'll keep for you the same affection, tenderness, respect and friendship I've had for so many years.

Pablo

She didn't answer. She didn't want to know any more. She refused to talk about the poet. She silenced everyone who tried to speak ill of him.

Pablo Neruda's attitude was tremendously criticized. The group that had been together for so many years divided forever. Tomás Lago, his closest friend, was the most drastic; he would never agree to meet Neruda again in his life. No doubt there'd been other factors, other arguments that had led to this conclusion. The separation was also a pretext for those who had old resentments to settle.

The first time Delia confronted the social world alone was on March 4, at the wedding of Victoria Lago, the daughter of Tomás and Irma Falcón. She and Pablo had been asked to be godparents. He sent an apology along with a gift, some antique cruets. She attended the ceremony, and at some point wandered away to the bedrooms. Someone found her distractedly reading a newspaper.

Each passing day enlarged the magnitude of the deception she'd been living through. The specific and painful details emerged. "I thought he didn't need it anymore," she answered a girlfriend, who was surprised to learn they hadn't had sexual relations for many years.

Delia was in the ambiguous situation of both not wanting to know and being morbidly curious to find out everything. Graciela knew too much. The unbearable truth went back to their days of exile in Mexico. Six whole years. All that time gave itself to second readings. A brutal blow.

The only solution, the obvious remedy, was to put distance between herself and these humiliating revelations.

With wounded pride, with a toughness bordering on arrogance, she found the courage to justify her own existence, and keep moving forward.

At the end of March she left for Buenos Aires. She'd advised the Alberti couple that she was coming. They waited for her at the airport, along with Margarita Aguirre and Rodolfo Aráoz Alfaro. They found her calm, and not as depressed as they'd expected. She asked to stay at the home of the Alberti couple, but they had no space. Against her wishes, secretly furious, she settled into the Aráoz Alfaro couple's apartment on Sánchez de Bustamante Street. Two days later, she left on a boat for Europe. They dropped her off in the morning at the dock in La Boca, but the boat delayed its departure until the evening. Delia took the opportunity to write a strongly worded letter to Margarita and Rodolfo, telling them off for having supported Pablo's deceit, leaving her exposed to ridicule. The letter also raged against all those who had called themselves friends, Jorge Amado, Diego Rivera and a great many more.

This venting was necessary to soothe the pain and gather the strength to begin a new stage.

CHAPTER 11

1956–1981

Although Paris was full of memories too, leaving Santiago, the center of the storm, lifted Delia's spirits. Her mixture of tenacity—"I'm a brute Basque," she'd say—and distraction helped her to regain a measure of normality. The episode was relegated to silence, submerged in secrecy, even if it was impossible to forget. She continued to avoid talking about what had happened. "I'm a dove with a wounded wing," she wrote to Aída Figueroa with a hint of irony, conscious of using a well-worn metaphor.

When recounting the legend of these days, some speak of a telegram or letter that Neruda sent to Paris, asking Delia to return, telling her again she'd always be the queen of the house. If such a communication exists, then there was no answer, and it didn't alter her decision in the slightest.

The natural thing to do was to return to painting, to the medium that had always been a pastime. Frequently interrupted, eternally postponed in favor of other events, it now reappeared as a necessary activity.

Nemesio Antúnez had talked to her about an engraving workshop that William Hayter directed in Paris. She'd met Bill Hayter in Madrid when she'd been his interpreter, during his enlistment in the Republican militia.

Workshop 17, located at that number on Rue Campagne Manier near Raspail Boulevard, had been dismantled, with its presses melted down during the German occupation. Hayter moved to New York and set up a similar workshop there. Back in Paris he set up on Rue Joseph Bara, so close to the original address that he decided to keep the name.

It was a small, simple studio with two presses, famous for its quality. Hayter had worked as a chemical engineer in Iran before dedicating himself to engraving, and now the most important artists went to him to print their works.

The Chilean painter Enrique Zañartu worked as an assistant to Hayter during those years, and he remembers helping the Ant with the technical aspects of her first prints. "Not out of friendship, simply to avoid catastrophe. She was capable of sticking her hand into acid, she wasn't aware of the danger of things. I was the victim of her enchantment. She functioned purely on *charme*. 'My son, how can I make huge prints like these? My son, find out how I can get this effect.' In that way she was able to advance in her work."

The strength required to grapple with the metal sheets was exactly what she needed, a way to use all of her energy. The physical and mental exertion helped to overcome her sadness.

Among these first engravings is a series with the suggestive title *El cisne levanta sus alas* [The Swan Raises Its Wings], which repeats with variations in other works. Another interesting series is called *Vida, pasión y muerte de una rosa* [Life, Passion and Death of a Rose], and features several engravings of a flower at different moments. One can appreciate her filigree work on the metal, which leaves no space unadorned.

If enthusiasm was one of her distinguishing qualities, here she exercised it with an incredible vitality. Her only plan was to progress in her work, moving forward, composing new ideas, leaving no time for nostalgia. In a strange way, everything seemed to reorient toward the future. The past didn't interest her, and even family matters, which some friends forced her to recall, went without a reply. She was always talking about her own plans, about the future of her own work.

After a year, she returned to Chile. Her house and friends were there. One might think it was the last place she would have wanted to go. She needed courage to make the journey, but she didn't have the slightest doubt about her decision.

The Ant arrived in Santiago with her engravings under her arm, full of projects. Her white hair, undyed and combed into a long mane, gave her a spontaneous air, and although she still painted her eyes black and her lips and cheeks red, her face looked calmer than it had during the difficult times.

It was gossiped that Pablo was issuing private invitations to friends who hadn't taken a clear side in the squall, in the hopes they would become friends with Matilde. But it was a losing battle, as sympathy wasn't one of the new Señora Neruda's attributes. In comparison with Delia, she came across badly. "He swapped the soul for the belly," was one of the gentler comments. But the Ant didn't hear any of this. She already knew who was on her side. The topic of Pablo Neruda was shut down. People who approached her to put down the poet met with her complete silence, and left confused.

Settling in Chile again was complicated. The Lynch house, which belonged to her, had been leased out by the Party, and a school was operating there. Looking for a quick solution, she settled into the elegant Crillón Hotel downtown.

Delia also owned the house at Isla Negra, the poet's favorite. This small house had expanded over the years, transforming into a large building due to Neruda's architectural zeal. The Party had to use its power as an organization to intervene with red tape, and make her sell it. She did so in October 1956, not to Neruda, but to the Party, represented by Luis Enrique Délano and Hernán Sanhueza Donoso.

The first thing she did upon returning was to sign up for Nemesio Antúnez's Workshop 99, named for its number on Guardia Vieja Street, like Hayter's workshop where she had practiced engraving.

Classes took place on Tuesdays and Wednesdays for the entire afternoon, in two small rooms separated by a patio where the students worked as a community. Nemesio Antúnez was the technical director, but all the students collaborated. When Delia joined, she found not only companionship but also firm friendships. Roser Bru, who had arrived on the *Winnipeg*, already knew her. When they'd run into each other in the street, the Ant had told her: "You should paint, darling, you must dedicate yourself to that." Now they were together in their work. For the Ant, these people—Roser Bru, Dinora Doudschitzky, Luz Donoso and Eduardo Vilches—represented a network of unconditional support in her new life, which she approached like a young student.

As in Paris, she unfurled all her charm to solicit the necessary help with the metal sheets. She would easily forget that she'd left her work in acid, and the solution would begin to heat until

Patricia Nazar, Dinora Doudschitzky and Delia. Gallery opening at Galería Central de Arte, 1968.

terrible yellow fumes began to emerge. The entire group would have to come to her rescue.

"What happens is that if you leave the sheet in acid for a long time, the plaque perforates. But she continued to work on it, because she found a way to make use of everything. She was clever and planned things to a certain degree, then left the rest to fate. She had a lot of intuition and knew how to take advantage of chance to benefit the work. She'd begin from a stain, something accidental in the engraving she was making, which wasn't hard for her because she was imaginative. She'd complain that it was difficult for her, that she didn't know academic drawing, but she did know what she wanted to express, and that's why her work has strength. She made her intentions concrete in the material. She was very bold, she had no fear..." Eduardo Vilches remembers.

Delia always contributed a tray of cakes at teatime. She herself didn't indulge, but stayed immersed in her drawings. "You all go drink tea, I don't have time." It was her only reference to the generational difference that separated her from her classmates.

She had enough energy to try her hand at business endeavors. Since there were almost no art galleries in Santiago, except for those managed by the Chilean-North American Institute and the Bank of Chile, she convinced Delia Solimano, Tomás Lago's wife, who owned a flower shop called Pamela's Garden, to set one up, taking advantage of her connections with new artists. *Sol de Bronce* [Bronze Sun], opened at the corner of Amunátegui and Catedral Street. There were exhibitions by the members of the workshop, and several engravings and drawings were sold. Whether due to the location, the lack of public interest or the inexperience of the owners, the gallery had a short life.

The Ant wanted to recover her house at all costs. She'd spent over a year living at the Crillón, and her paperwork with the Communist Party hadn't advanced. Naturally, she needed someone else to worry about taking concrete action. And as always, someone appeared. Delia went one Sunday with Luz Donoso and Juan García Huidobro to Viña Santa Rita, and she fell in love with the place, with its big park and enormous house. When she saw horses feeding at a manger, she insisted on riding. The group saddled them and took a turn around the park, but her friends didn't let her gallop, as she'd have liked. Admiring the landscape, she complained about spending so much time shut away in a hotel room, missing her garden. Juan García Huidobro offered to resolve the matter for her. It wouldn't be easy, as he had to find a place for the forty children settled at Lynch. But within a few months there was news. They'd returned the house to her. Her contacts had come through.

Luz and Juan helped her with the move, retrieving the few possessions still scattered at friends' houses: a pair of lilac curtains, a sofa bed with an attached bookcase, a grand piano, a few items of furniture. An aquarium had been left in the living room of the house, facing the garden, along with a box of butterflies. Neruda had taken the rest.

The house was a mess, its walls dirty, its plumbing broken, the roof in terrible shape. But Delia was delighted. Her only concern was that she'd be left alone that night, without music. She begged her friends to immediately buy her a radio, and then she was satisfied.

The Lynch house continued to adapt. It took on a different, calmer life. Friends came to visit, and many settled in for a time.

Ramón González, an architect and Party member married to Sonia Muñoz—the daughter of Diego Muñoz and Regina Falcón, who had become friends with Delia during the period of persecution by González Videla—came to live at Lynch, and helped her with the administration of the house.

The room where she'd set up a workshop years before was her most important space. Nobody could enter except her, and she'd work vigorously for many hours, entire afternoons.

On Saturdays, she had lunch with artist friends. People from the workshop and visitors from abroad all went to her famous lunches. Somebody might play the piano, another sing, but conversation was the main feature. The pisco sour was Delia's drink of choice, and she always thought the food was incredible, a miracle. She never quite realized how everything came together around her.

On Sundays she received other visits. Before lunch the writer José Santos González Vera might appear, and they would chat for hours. Or it might be the poet Juvencio Valle, or her neighbors Margarita and Alejandro Lipschutz. Once in a blue moon, the writer Manuel Rojas would come, and they'd get involved in tremendous political discussions. Rojas was a Trotskyist, or rather an anarchist, totally anti-Stalin. When the discussion grew heated she'd say: "Let's see, say there's a war between the United States and the Soviet Union. Who are you for?" Manuel Rojas, who always carried swear words on the tip of his tongue, would answer: "Cursing, I'd pick the Soviet Union." And she'd be satisfied.

In the afternoons Tomás Lago, Delia Solimano, Graciela Matte and others interested in politics stopped by. Delia stayed informed. She read the newspapers, especially *El Siglo*, which she knew by heart. Everyone says she continued to give her opinion on the most varied topics with enormous accuracy, despite her blind faith in communism, even in the face of Nikita Khrushchev's revelations and criticisms of Stalinist excess.

Delia's life in those years was a jigsaw with pieces from different worlds, which began to fit together in various ways, slotting her into her surroundings. She brought together the characters and friendships of the past with the fierce and spontaneous nature that she enjoyed in young people, and her presence gave rise to warm and genuine connections. Perhaps in a subtle way, she imposed an unquestioning loyalty on her visitors that eased her independent existence and hid the depths of her heartbreak.

The women around her—Roser Bru, Dinora Doudschitzky, Ida González, Inés Valenzuela, Aída Figueroa, Irene Domínguez, Amalia Chaigneau—were loyal and concerned friends, always available, but it must be said that the Ant preferred the men. With them she felt approval, certainty. She practiced flirtation, enchantment and seduction, in clear need of reaffirmation; establishing herself as an equal, she showed that being a woman didn't diminish her in any way. It was obvious to her that men dominated the world. In an interview, she said: "In society, woman is still an inferior in her condition, and man struggles to maintain this position of hers. Just as the Chinese would put special shoes on women so they didn't go out in the street, so Western man invented other 'Chinese shoes' for her, so as not to lose his control... If you become a feminist, they get rid of you."

In women she found support; in men she sought recognition.

After a short time, Workshop 99 moved to the central building of the Catholic University on the Alameda, a fourth floor that could be accessed by climbing endless stairs. Delia took the bus at Egaña Plaza and went there twice a week.

Work was the central axis of her life. In 1959 a horse appeared for the first time in one of her prints. It was a simple little horse, almost a toy, with a man riding it. The figure gave her a profound emotional shock. She didn't understand it. The theme, which echoed her past, was a sign. It burst through like a revelation, a sudden discovery of what was her own.

She titled it *El caballero sin inconvenientes* [The Rider Without Worries]. Usually she liked to invent her own names for her prints, but this one, which she'd discovered in a poem by Juvencio Valle, was a perfect fit.

She struggled with the complicated technique of printmaking, due to her bold use of the chisel, her desire for spaciousness that exceeded the limited area of the metal sheets, and her insistence on intense blacks and whites that were difficult to reproduce in copies. Her companions suggested a change in technique. She started to make big drawings on paper with charcoal.

The success of Workshop 99, where more than twenty-five artists worked, coincided with the opening of a gallery, the Central de Arte, directed by Carmen Waugh. There Delia's prints of horses were exhibited and sold. The results exceeded all expectations. Such prints became fashionable, and copies were sold by the hundreds. Del Carril, along with Antúnez, Vilches, Bru, Santos Chávez and Millar, hung on the walls of Chilean bourgeoisie, avant-gardes and conservatives alike. They were the most refined and universal gift. A phenomenon.

For Delia, exhibiting and selling her work was a recognition that she hadn't anticipated. After so many attempts and so much work, she was considered an artist.

The Ant devised an infallible system to carry out her will. According to Roser Bru, she used collective thinking to convince everyone of what she wished to do. "Friends say…" was her recurring phrase when some idea got into her head. "Friends say I should go to Paris again, they're crazy, you know, they've convinced me I must go."

She went on the trip in 1960. She took along Joan Morrison, a young artist who was living at Lynch. Not only had she taken a room there, but she was the one who organized the famous Saturday lunches and helped Delia for years with all her needs. "Joan," the Ant would call out, and Joan had to arrange her hair, put blush on her cheeks, and paint her eyes and lips, since without her glasses Delia might have applied a ridiculous amount.

Joan recalls the week they were together in Paris as a permanent coming and going, to concerts, to visit Hayter, to attend a Picasso exhibition, and to meet with the artist himself, where she was impressed by his familiarity with Delia as they swapped jokes and traded ironic, witty phrases. Walks by the Seine, where the Ant began to run with joy. Lunches at La Coupole, remembering Joan's mother who had met Delia in another time, at a party in Michoacán where Bola de Nieve sang during his visit to Chile.

From her stays at Lynch over a period of twenty years, Joan Morrison recalls Delia's long conversations with visitors who would later emerge in importance. These included Nicolás Guillén; Doris Dana, the literary executor of Gabriela Mistral; Joris Ivens, the Dutch documentary maker; Dominique, the widow of Paul Éluard; and Victoria Ocampo, who renewed her friendship with Delia after she distanced herself from Neruda.

The poet had gone too far in attacking the magazine *Sur* and Victoria with a poem collected in his book *The Grapes and the Wind*: "Thorns and abruptness protected / your terrible misery, / while Mme. Charmante / yammered French in the salons. / The whip fell / on the scars of your people, / while the elegant litterateurs / at her magazine *Sur* (surely) / studied Lawrence the spy, / or Heidegger or 'notre petit Drieu' (…) *Oui Madame*, what a world / has left us, what an irreparable / loss for all / the distinguished people!" (from "Dedos quemados" [Burnt Fingers]). Coincidentally or not, the poem dates to the period when his marriage to Delia was on the rocks.

Daily life for the Ant included ten hours at the workshop; time in the garden, tended by Eduardo Vilches, which she believed was a miracle of nature; the selling of avocados, walnuts, persimmons and almonds when money was short; a disorder of clothes and papers; and long spiels against baroque music.

At the end of 1962, she left for Paris to work at Hayter's workshop again. She lived with Gigy López in her apartment on Rue de Grenelle, just like when she'd stayed with her after escaping Chile in 1955. She surprised this girlfriend with her high spirits, and every morning could be heard singing in the bathroom at the top of her lungs.

Her silence about Neruda was broken, now that she was far away from Chile. A few years had passed, and she could talk about her disillusionment openly, saying that her pain had been due to the deception and lies, and that she felt swindled. What was unforgivable was the disloyalty. Maybe, if things had happened some other way, she'd have been able to understand.

"This is Delia, a very close friend of mine from Spain. She's come from Chile and I beg you to help her, to look after her, because every time she comes she leaves me with tremendous disasters," Hayter told his new assistant, another Chilean named Eugenio Téllez. Eugenio became Delia's chaperone and guide. She would confuse the aquatint with the alcohol, and of course she had trouble lifting the giant metal sheets she worked with. She was preparing some prints, a few illustrations for the *Song of Songs*, which would be published in Chile. She drew horses that took on an unbridled ferocity, spilling over the margins, fragmented and all the more dynamic for not being complete. Their flared nostrils and almost human gaze made them unique; nobody could find a comparison. They had something reminiscent of Romanesque or primitive horses, like drawings on stone.

"What are you doing here, my son, you're very young, how are things going for you, how do you manage?" Delia always expressed concern for her assistant, who helped her out of tight spots. For him, the friendship meant an introduction to a different side of Paris, with long outings, visits, lunches at La Coupole and the nearby bistro, and trips to the cinema. This was how she, without great fuss, in her delicate way, returned the favor for his support.

From France she went to Moscow, as a Women's Association had invited her to show her works, a reward from the Party to its faithful follower.

She returned to Chile. The Lynch house served as a refuge for the children of friends who wanted more independence or had separated from their partners, leaving them without a place to stay. A few activists from the Party lived there too. The house held frequent fundraisers for communist activities. Even the inhabitants had to pay an entrance fee. It was an unusual house, open to both public and private life.

Her income continued to dwindle as home maintenance grew complicated. During the winter the cold was intense, and only the Ant's ironclad health enabled her to pay no attention to it.

Some girlfriends proposed she should sell the house. What she obtained from the sale would be enough to settle into a comfortable apartment with money to spare.

Amalia Chaigneau and Roser Bru took it upon themselves to talk with an agent and initiate the process. When they were about to close the transaction, during the bustle of paperwork, they discovered that the house had been donated to the Party in 1971. Everything continued as before.

"My son, I'm so sad, they're going to sell the house," she said to Jorge Palacios, who then suggested she rent out her rooms to him. He settled into what had been Neruda's library on the second floor, where he'd kept his snails. The lease would keep the Ant in glory and majesty.

But the matter didn't end well. Palacios was one of the founders of the Spartacus group, the Pekinist line that opposed Moscow and adhered to the Maoist Cultural Revolution.

When Luis Corvalán, the General Secretary of the Party, informed Delia that these revolutionary dissidents had gathered at her house, she thought it was a mistake: "It isn't possible, he's such a good man, I have faith in him..." But the evidence was overwhelming. Angry and upset, she asked him to leave.

Delia, who overflowed with vitality and never rested, and who kept the exact figure of her age a secret, avoiding the inquiries of friends who discovered the dates on her passports and identity cards didn't match, now turned eighty years old.

A useless discussion about whether her fall was the cause of the break, or if the hip broke on its own and made her fall to the ground, took place around Delia in the hallway of the building where Graciela Matte lived, one afternoon at the weekly lunch.

She couldn't believe it. It was a complete fiasco, an atrocity she'd never considered, just as she hadn't thought of death because she was prepared for immortality, absurd as it may have sounded.

Unable to move, lying in a room of the Traumatological Hospital, she was open to anything that could restore her to health. An operation, irons, bolts to keep her walking. "Dancing, doctor, do you think I'll be able to dance?"

Doctor Héctor Orrego Puelma, her great friend and former neighbor at Isla Negra, visited her. And he brought her a surprise. He wanted to read to her from Neruda's latest book which had just appeared, called *Memorial de Isla Negra* [Isla Negra: A Notebook]. He said there was a beautiful poem dedicated to her.

"No, Titín, by no means, I don't want to know about that."

But he insisted, as he was sure it would be comforting to her. And he read out loud:

Delia is the light from the window / open to truth, to the tree of honey, / and time passed without me knowing / if there remained from badly wounded years / only her radiance of intelligence, / the gentleness with which she accompanied / my pains, in difficult abiding.

Because to judge by what I remember / where the seven swords were sunk / into me, looking for blood, / and absence flowed from my heart, / there, Delia, the luminous moon / of your reason swept aside my sorrows.

You, from the vast land / reached me / with a vast heart, spread out / like golden grain, open / to the transmigrations of flour / and there's no tenderness like that which falls / as the rain falls in the meadow: / slow come the drops, received by / space, manure, silence / and the awakening of cattle / which low in the damp under the violin / of the sky.

From there / like the scent left by a rose / in mourning dress, in winter / so I recognized you at once / as if you'd always been mine / without being so, without more than that naked / trace or clear shadow / of petal or luminous sword.

The war arrived then: / you and I received it at the door: / it seemed a transient virgin / who sang dying / and the smoke, the blast / of blue powder on the snow / looked beautiful / but all at once / there were our broken windows, / the shrapnel / between the books, / the fresh blood / in puddles on the streets: / war isn't smiles, / the anthems slept, / the ground trembled at the heavy step / of the soldier, / death threshed / grain after grain: / our friend didn't return, / that hour / was bitter without crying / later, later the tears, / because it was honor that cried, / maybe in defeat / we didn't know / the most immense grave was opening up / and nations and cities / would fall into earth. / That age is our scars. / We keep the sadness and ashes.

Now there they go / through the gate / of Madrid, / the Moors. / Franco arrives in his carriage of skeletons, / our friends / dead and exiled.

Delia, amidst so many leaves / from the tree of life, / your presence / in the fire, / your virtue / of dew: / a dove / in the furious wind.

* * *

The peoples fell silent and slept / each time one was and will be: / maybe it wasn't resentment that was born in you, / because it's written where it can't be read / that spent love is not death / but a bitter form of being born.

Forgive me for my heart, / inhabited by a great buzzing of bees: / I know you, like all beings, / will touch the sublime honey / and break away from the lunar stone / of the firmament / your own star, / you, crystalline among women.

I do not scorn, I feel no contempt, I am / a treasurer of the sea, I barely hear / damaging words, / and I rebuild / my room, my science, my joy, / if only I could add the sadness / of my absent eyes, / but neither reason nor madness / were for me: / I loved again, and love rose up / as a wave in my life and I went filled / by love, only love, / without intending anyone unhappiness.

For that reason, / most gentle passenger, / thread of steel and honey who tied my hands / through the echoing years / you exist as not a vine / on a tree but with your own truth.

I will pass, we will pass, / says the water / and sings the truth against the stone, / the riverbed spills over and branches away, / the mad grasses grow / on the bank: / I will pass, we will pass, / says night to day / month to year, / time / granting an integrity to the testimony / of those who lose, and those who gain / but tirelessly the tree grows / and the tree dies and life yields / another germ, and everything goes on.

And it's not adversity that separates / beings, but / growth, / and a flower never dies: it keeps on being born.

For that reason, although forgive me / as I forgive / and he's guilty and she / and they come and go / those tongues tied / to bafflement and shamelessness, / the truth / is that / everything has blossomed / and the sun doesn't know scars.

(poems later printed as "Amores: Delia (I)" and "Amores: Delia (II)" [Loves: Delia (I) and Loves: Delia (II)], in *Isla Negra: A Notebook*)

Delia was silent for a long time.

"How lovely. What a pity it's by Pablo and dedicated to me."

It was her only comment.

Everyone thought that this accident, this fall, would be the end of Delia, that she wouldn't recover. But after two months, she was already trying to walk, insisting the sessions with the physical therapists should be more frequent, and longer. She became obsessed with healing.

Soon she picked up her drawing again, setting up a gigantic stand in the bedroom onto which Eduardo Vilches had to clip the papers on. "You do such a good job of hanging up the pages for me, my son." Ida González was responsible for the purchases of French paper from the National Library. One page had to be added to another when the horses grew larger than a single sheet, respecting no margin.

The task of erasure was another job for the community in which everybody participated. Many erasers were bought, and Delia led the operation. There were a few people she trusted fully for this, Irene Domínguez, Eduardo Vilches, Ida González. The marks the eraser left were fixed with a razor blade and chalk, delicate work she approved step by step. If she didn't like someone, she'd say: "He's no good even for erasing."

The invitation to exhibit in Buenos Aires at the Lirolay Gallery, near the end of 1965, was a new experience. For the first time she'd be going to her country as an artist. It was a challenge and a source of pride. She was worried about the reactions of her many acquaintances, such as María Rosa Oliver and especially Victoria Ocampo, who had somehow never considered Delia to be capable of producing serious artwork.

Here's a letter in which she discusses how it went:

Dec 15, 1965. My beloved Workshop 99: Love, love, love!!! Our letters crossed. I didn't have time to answer your collective message, because here everything requires an enormous effort. Today your new letter got here, Roser! I'm working for an active Chilean-Argentine exchange. I have the offer of Lirolay Hall for Santos Chávez (let him know) from March 7 to March 19, or March 21 to April 2. Even though everyone comes to this gallery, I haven't dared request anything else. Let me tell you my experience, and you can decide. They invited me. If I hadn't sold anything, I'd have had to leave some of my work as a courtesy, but since I did sell, I'll give thirty percent, as is usual in all the galleries. They've invited Santos under the same conditions. The Gallery charged my charming friend Pop Art but soon it'll fly with its own wings. My first buyers were Chilean friends, the drawing of the two horses where it's not clear whether it has one or two heads, and after them some Argentines, two prints with the same theme, *El caballo y la caballita* [The Horse and the Pony] and now you stop counting. Later I sold the other two with the heads twined together, an eye for an eye, a tooth for a tooth, to the representatives of the New York Times. They came to replace what they had until now and also bought *Hara Kiri*—you remember, Roser, you named it. *Al que murió de espanto* [To the One Who Died of Fright] was purchased by the Argentine National Endowment for the Arts, along with *Lágrima viva* [Living Tear.] I'm convinced the Chileans are going to have a great success, we'll talk when I'm back. There's a lot of Pop Art even in the fabric of women's dresses, because—as Guillermo Nuñez said in the forum that opened an Argentine exhibition—the Argentines plunge in, while the Chileans show an excessive reserve. The reason (for me) that Pop Art is celebrated by the public is that it was never a revolution in art. Neither the Impressionists, nor the Cubists, nor the Surrealists, nor Dada had the acceptance the shrieks

and howls of current music and painting have today. The reason
is that they came from the revolt of a few visionaries, but today
represent a rebellion on behalf of the entire dreadful existence
of an increasing number of people. What I mean is, what was
the expression of a select minority before now belongs to an
immense majority, unsatisfied and frustrated. Kisses and hugs
from Delia. I'll travel on December 28 or 29. Ramo [Adelina del
Carril's adopted son] has asked me to spend Christmas here.

After she got back, and despite her difficulties walking, she
insisted on a totally normal life, going out, attending exhibitions
and listening to concerts by the Symphonic Orchestra, to which
she was a subscriber. Since she couldn't get up during the inter-
vals, people would come to greet her at her seat, gathering around.
Nor did she stop going to Graciela Matte's lunches, or for her
weekly visits to the house of Sergio Insunza and Aída Figueroa.

The Insunza couple was, in many ways, her family. She spent
summers by their side at Quintero Beach, celebrated Christmas
with them and never missed a birthday. She treated their children
like she treated all young people, as her equals, worrying about
their interests and what they'd do in life, and encouraging any
inclination she perceived. Ramiro Insunza was her companion
and friend in many activities. If there was a concert that especially
interested her, she'd call him, and he'd pick her up in his jeep.
Delia, wearing a handkerchief on her head, enjoyed the adventure.
Ramiro would park the car in front of the theater entrance and
lift her into his arms, carrying her to her seat. "You're completely
crazy, Ramiro," she'd tell him, delighted by the view. She gave him
lectures, too. "You can be different after you do everything else,"
she declared, trying to convince him not to abandon his studies
in architecture.

During a summer holiday in Quintero, she was on the verge of running into Pablo and Matilde, who'd come to greet their friends. She had to perform all kinds of maneuvers to avoid the meeting. Aída took her away in the car, inventing an urgent trip to Viña del Mar.

Sergio Insunza was responsible for delivering Pablo's request to annul the marriage. At first, she flatly refused. She didn't want to hear about it. After months of convincing, of long and tense conversations, she accepted, so long as she wouldn't have to participate directly in the proceedings. She gave power of attorney to Luis Cuevas Mackenna. But she had to personally receive the notification of the claim, sign it, and present her identity card n°1757530 in Santiago. She had to face reality.

On June 16, 1966, sentence was passed in favor of the plaintiff Pablo Neruda in the trial of matrimonial annulment brought against Delia del Carril Iraeta.

"You know I don't want to talk about that, love, those twenty years are erased, they don't exist," she answered a journalist, interviewing her about her work. As always, he tried to ask about her relationship with the poet.

They ran into each other more than once.

At Mario Carreño's big exhibition at the University of Chile, everyone was nervous, except for her. Pablo had arrived with Matilde. Afterward there would be a meal at Miria Contreras's house. Friends surrounded Delia. "He knows what he's doing, I'm an artist and with my artist friends," she said. Miria Contreras took her by car. They were the first to arrive at the house, and they settled into the living room. The next to walk in were Pablo and Matilde. An enormous minute passed in complete silence before the other guests arrived.

Months later, Santiago Aguirre celebrated his sixtieth birthday with a party at his spacious apartment on Santa María Avenue. He'd organized the birthday in secret, inviting all his friends, the old group from so many years before that had scattered due to quarrels, matrimonial separations and troubles of every kind. Along with his friend Carlos Vasallo, he'd titled the gathering "El Desgenéresis", using the name of a work of theater being staged at the time at the University of Chile. The Ant arrived with Delia Solimano and Tomás Lago. Late in the evening, when the party seemed to have avoided the scandal that the organizers were hoping for, Pablo and Matilde arrived. The chaos was complete. The group closed ranks around the Ant, and Tomás Lago furiously pulled the owner of the house aside. Pablo and Matilde moved to the terrace. Graciela Álvarez brought everyone whisky to calm the mood. It was a staging of the great schism that still divided the old bohemians, eighteen years later.

The hip operation didn't turn out well. Despite her efforts and the daily attendance of physical therapists who subjected her to exercises—which she transformed with humor into strange dances—it remained difficult for her to walk and move, and the work with her drawings was especially hard going. She spent many hours in her room, and her exasperation at her disability made her increasingly demanding. The people around her changed. They would leave her side for work, marriage, travel and other unavoidable engagements, but others always arrived. Even after so many years, the Ant remained a lodestar, entertaining those who flocked to her.

Her great-nephew in Chile, Gabriel del Carril, the son of Conrado and Marta Amunátegui, occupied a place of honor. He arrived with his friends from school, played soccer in the enormous garden and bandits in the backyard theater now in ruins, and then came inside to watch television and drink tea with her, accompanied by toast with avocado, an essential in that house. He was Delia's only remaining link with the family she'd left behind in Argentina, whose deaths she had experienced from afar.

In 1967 she learned of the death of Adelina. Marta Amunátegui heard the news and gathered the strength to tell her. She went with Tomás Lago. When they arrived, Delia was having tea with Gracia Barrios and José Balmes. Marta drew her aside and gave her the news. Delia only said: "Let's go back and finish our tea." When everyone had left, she surrendered to her sadness. She'd shared so much with her sister, and they'd always been so united.

> Dear María Rosa (Oliver), Sarita (Jorge): What a shame it's with sad news you write to me at last, because of the so unexpected death of Adelina, whom we all knew was fatally marked. I watched over Ricardo, my sister Julia, and also Mario, another brother of mine, at the end, and I told myself that although we're all condemned to death, if we arrive at this death working, fighting and even singing, as Adelina did with the child Ramo, we're all just the same. And then comes the pang in the chest, brutal, contradictory, to ask why her and not me. I wrote to Ramo and to Lucía, her mother-in-law, the one who's always kept me informed, and for whom I feel an enormous gratitude and affection. I'm happy that a person like this is by her side, what one can truly call by her side. You're right, María Rosa, Ramo was the best Adelina had in the last stage of her life. But what will become of him now… I write this and begin to cry. I'd like you to let him know that you understand him, and recognize his true grief. Believe me, I worry about him as much as you do. I can't grasp that with all her affection Adelina hasn't done anything concrete in practical matters. I

don't know if you're aware that when he came from India, she thought she'd adopted him because she brought a letter about him authorizing her to bring him to Buenos Aires. The international police told her the letter wasn't worth anything, and that Ramo couldn't arrive in Buenos Aires or disembark from the boat. She kicked up an immense scandal with cries and screams, and Ramo got off with her. To me she said that Ramo hadn't consented to be adopted and that her lawyer José María Lamarca had told her it wasn't necessary to make a will in his favor. Check if this is the case. It was the year I was living on Martínez Street, in '66. I know she considered him to be her son and would suffer terribly if all of us didn't consider him as such. But she was like those Catholics, and I include myself but only when I was a very small girl, who laughed about civil marriage and thought of it as a carnival. Sarita, you once did me the kindness of coming to my house, and to you, María Rosa, I give my thanks, as I do to all the dear Bortagarai family, as well as to Pancho and Leonor for their affectionate memories. I can't travel due to lack of money. My exhibition, though it made a lot of noise, was pure expenses to buy huge sheets of glass, and my human topics aren't as pleasant as my horses, which are highly sought after by the Chileans. Now Chile will send me to the Biennale in Quito with its young painters. I continue to work tirelessly, and I send you all lots of love. Delia. PS. María Rosa, if you could ever resign yourself to coming with Sarita to Lynch, which has a great deal of space, I'd die of happiness...

The turnover of people at the Lynch house, and the need for money to maintain it, made those close to Delia keep an out eye for possible renters. Any possible contender had to fulfill a few additional requirements too, so there'd be no problems getting along with Delia's way of life.

Military dictatorships in Latin America were at their peak. Brazil, Uruguay and Argentina, under the authoritarianism of Juan Carlos Onganía, were living through repressive governments. The youths, the students, suffered the worst. Chile, in those years, was a democracy where they could take refuge.

At the University of Chile, Amalia Chaigneau met a couple that seemed like perfect renters: two young, intelligent, political Argentines who'd come from the University of Córdoba, Mabel Piccini and Carlos Sempat. They agreed to go meet the Ant, to see if they passed the test to settle in with her.

She received them and they talked about politics, history—Sempat was already a reputable historian—music and art, everything but money. She showed them the house as if she were giving them a tour, explaining its rooms and how it was constructed, without special emphasis, without looking for any agreement.

They didn't think the matter had come to anything, but a few days later they met with Amalia. "The Ant was delighted with you, she's expecting you, you can move in whenever you like."

What most caught their attention was that the two doors of the house, those of the front gate and the main entrance, were always left open. They were only closed very late at night.

Continuing the tradition, each renter led an independent life while sharing in parties, drinks and friendships that jumbled generations, ideologies and convictions. The open doors perfectly symbolized the collective environment of the house. Anyone could come in. The neighborhood dogs strolled through the living room.

Delia's breakfast was light, and she ate little when she was alone. But when the time came for parties, or for the Friday meals that replaced the famous Saturday lunches, she enjoyed the shared food and drank pisco sours and wine along with everyone.

"She had an immense tolerance," said Mabel. "She was beyond good and evil. There was never an argument or any trouble; she wanted to live and be happy."

Delia's great dream, now an obsession, was to exhibit in Paris. "Friends say I should go to Paris and show my pictures." The one responsible for helping her to fulfill her desire was Emilio Ellena. Since the end of 1964, when he'd met her, Emilio had been Delia's great friend and manager. A mathematician, collector and expert in prints, he was a devoted admirer of her work. And he paid the price—he always had to be prepared to arrange her travels, and worry over both large-scale projects and tiny details to achieve the impossible for her. The trip to Paris was one of his biggest challenges.

To leave the country, she always faced the significant problems of someone who doesn't understand paperwork, and has never heard of the organizations that regulate daily life. Every trip was an adventure. "What does this lady live on?" an incredulous public servant asked, checking her papers before one of her quick trips to Buenos Aires. "Miracles," was the only thing that Roser Bru, who accompanied her, could think to say.

Getting ready for Paris, the international vaccination certificate didn't appear. "How old is the lady?" the civil servant asked. "Eighty-three," she replied, for once not shaving off a few years. "Then you don't need the paper." "My son, this is the first time my age has been useful for anything."

They arrived in Paris on the same Sunday in April 1969 as the "No" referendum against General Charles de Gaulle. The city was crowded and they had to lodge at different hotels. Her friend Madame Corot had reserved her a room at a residence for the elderly on St. Michel Boulevard. She couldn't bear it and phoned Emilio, asking him to change it as soon as possible.

The two of them spent a week together. Emilio returned to Chile and left the Ant in the hands of Irene Domínguez, who performed a juggling act to comply with Delia's requests and go on with her own life.

Another figure also assisted Irene with this challenging, arduous task: Adelita Gallo. The Ant had met her in the '40s in Chile, when Adelita was an active communist, driving trucks to transport workers. An intimate friend of Violeta Parra, the latter had accompanied her to Paris at the start of the '60s: "Old lady, sell your things and come with me, you can drive the pick-up." Violeta would meet one of the great loves of her life there, the Swiss clarinettist Gilbert Favre. Adelita was short and quite plump, with a keen sense of wit. Her friendship with Violeta's boyfriend unleashed the singer's jealousy. "You're flirting with my boyfriend, so I'm going to leave you on your own. Old lady, be a man," Violeta told her. This is how Adelita found herself in Paris at fifty-five years old, without being able to speak French. She made ends meet by baking empanadas until Irene Domínguez introduced her to Wifredo Lam. She worked for him as a perfect housekeeper, becoming an indispensable part of the family.

Delia's exhibition would take place in June, at the Josie Perón gallery-bookstore on Rue St. Placide. Someone had to help her set up the show, and Enrique Zañartu was prepared. He did everything. Delia was extremely anxious. For ten days she'd been completely blind: instead of the eye drops she'd been prescribed, she'd applied boric acid. Victoria Ocampo was in Paris. They'd eaten together, but Ocampo had continued her trip; she couldn't stay for the exhibition. Louis Aragon and Elsa Triolet had behaved badly and failed to attend many events, but they did promise to come to this inauguration.

Paris, Saturday, June 1969. Roser, Emilio, Sylvia, Mónica (González)—Flávian we will leave out of these ritual ceremonies—Nemesio, Khran, Palle, Vilches, Ortúzar and Dinora (those who come to mind). ALL ALL ALL should come to my Lynch house to take part in countless rites of exorcism to cast away evil spirits, walk barefoot on grass soaked in dew (mayonnaise), to purify themselves, and SING sing sing first at the top of their lungs, then slowly, more slowly, then very slowly, extremely slowly for a crazy Ant who has an exhibition in Paris at last after running through the whole spectrum of anguish, June 27 at the Josie Perón Librairie-Galerie, 7/3 Rue Saint Placide, Paris VI. Huge long kisses, Love Love Love Delia.

The Aragon couple went to the inauguration, and there was a note about the exhibition in *Le Figaro*, but Delia's secret illusions of leaping to fame were not fulfilled.

She wrote many letters to friends as a way of alleviating the discouragement and confusion she felt at being alone in a city where she could no longer handle herself with ease.

August 18, 1969. Dear Roser, Emilio, Dinora: In eleven days I leave for Buenos Aires. I go on August 29, 1969 at 10:20 at night, and arrive in BA on the 30th. Please, I trust in you most Roser, but I don't need letters only from you. I don't know what's going on with you Emilio, except what Lucho Cuevas and Sergio [Insunza] say. Please write immediately before I leave Paris. I promised my family to stay for longer in Buenos Aires, but I'm going into things not knowing what I'm doing. A girlfriend, one of the VERY ordered and practical ones, lost my address book, so I'm going to write to addresses from memory to announce my arrival. I'll write to Coppola to see where I can exhibit. Carlos Radich, Ximena Sotomayor's boyfriend (is he still?) knows the house number. If they send it to me in time, I can corroborate my chaotic letter with a message by night cable. I'm thinking of my trip, this time alone!!!!! Emilio might come a week early. He'd see two or three sensational things in Paris and the surroundings and accompany me through this difficult spell. I don't know if I told you about an exhibition at the Musée de l'Homme. Emilio, what's British Columbia? There are some huge totems that are very beautiful. Does it have anything to do with Colombia, like the Guyanas with Venezuela? Whatever the case, it's America. It was a revelation for me. I don't know if I managed to tell you that the increase of twenty-five percent in taxes along with the devaluation of the franc by twelve point something percent has all the French and foreigners very worried. In the meantime, those of us in my situation have to leave. My disability has been doubled because to the problem of my hip has been added that of my pocketbook, greatly limiting my movements. Hey Roserita, why don't you announce to Lucho (Cuevas) the sale of my horse so he calms down a bit, and so my friends can stop sending aid. I don't know anything about my lands in San Juan, they could help out somehow. Humanity is still in the age of the caves, and only reads the news about Ireland. While we're in possession of the most fabulous scientific successes, men think of nothing but killing—like spineless Mr. Nixon—mediocrity in all its glory and squalor. Don't leave me so lonely, you could already have answered my last collective letter, it's the only possible way for me. Where did you get the news, Emilio, that Gigy Lopez was in Paris? When I got here I asked after Eugenio Téllez but he was in the USA, and Wifredo Lam was in Italy, and Roberto Matta was also in Italy and so it went with everyone. I've seen Cecilia Bruna and Hernán Valdés, who interviewed me on the radio for Spain and Latin America. I think it was a failure and that they didn't transmit it, which makes me happy, even if Superville who directs the broadcast told me it was edited and transmitted. They didn't let me listen to find out if I'd approve of it. Everyone works from dawn to dusk, husbands and wives, for great salaries to afford life but little delight in living, and without the only things that can make us forget the surrounding disasters, like sacred friendship. Roser, please write and make them write! kisses kisses kisses to Roser, Emilio, Dinora and all my other friends. Delia.

In Buenos Aires she settled into a hotel at 183 Parera Street because she wanted to be near María Rosa Oliver, who was living nearby. On many afternoons she met with María Rosa and Victoria Ocampo, and the three rebellious women spoke about how they'd shaped their fates. They had all changed their lives, but while Victoria and María Rosa had transformed into institutions of culture and politics, Delia's form of freedom was more subtle, and occasionally elusive. Her arguments and thoughts would wander, and by the end of a serious talk, she'd say: "What I'd really like to do right now is go to a cabaret and dance." And her two friends would look at her with disapproval.

Tireless, she stayed incredibly active with friends, meals and cinemas, and complained that everyone else was too busy. On October 6, she opened another exhibition at Lirolay. She wrote to Chile requesting that her friends attend. Paris had disillusioned her, and she didn't want the same to happen in her city. Money was scarce. It was possible she'd finally sell the thousands of hectares of useless land in San Juan. Interested parties now appeared, hoping to mine the riches in her hills.

During one of the meals to which she was invited, she met María Teresa and Marcela Sola. Delia was making her case for the Soviet Union, and they started to discuss the matter. As it turned out, they were friends with María Rosa, and Delia later described how she converted the two to communism. The sisters were delighted by her personality and invited her to lunch. Delia finally went to live at María Teresa's house, relieving the stress on her finances, about which she hadn't said a word.

María Teresa Sola had to get used to Delia's exhausting rhythm, to the lunches that could last for three hours, to her mania of chewing a piece of meat eighty times. She would make plans from morning to night, and conversations would last until dawn.

"We have to buy tickets to go see him," said Delia when a concert by Vinicius de Moraes and Toquinho was announced. But on the day of the performance, María Rosa invited them for a whisky, because Vinicius was coming to visit. They spent time with him and went to the theater afterward. As always, there was a bottle of whisky and a lot of ice onstage to accompany the poet as he sang. Before finishing, he announced that this concert was dedicated to a great friend, a great woman who was in the audience, "the Ant" del Carril. Forgetting her limp, Delia climbed onstage and they hugged, as the audience enthusiastically applauded. She didn't sleep that night, fascinated by this gesture from a friend whom she hadn't seen for years.

She returned to Chile after having made a truly great effort. To exhibit in Paris and Buenos Aires, and to be able, after so many years, to introduce a work of her own and show herself as an artist, had been a way of presenting herself to people differently. She was no longer the aristocrat converted to communism, or the wife of the famous poet Pablo Neruda. This achievement was truly hers. But the world had changed, and it was naïve to hope for more.

In May she gave a retrospective exhibition at the Central Gallery of Art. Interviews appeared in newspapers and magazines, in which she continued to dodge personal questions about her marriage to Neruda. The critics also took up her work, some praising the quality of her enormous drawings and the impressive strength of her horses, others calling attention to her work as a printmaker. All of them agreed on the refinement of her craft and the elegance of her gaze, in which her expressive side powerfully surfaced: "The purity of Delia del Carril is the purity of pain, of human understanding, of compassion for her fellow creatures," said the critic from *El Mercurio*.

Chile prepared for presidential elections. The elderly candidate from the right, Jorge Alessandri, railed against the dangers of communism if Allende and Popular Unity triumphed; his hands shook visibly during the television broadcast. The government candidate, Radomiro Tomic, was just as unattractive, making a leftist victory less remote. At the Lynch house, the communists organized festivities to raise money, and Delia donated many prints for sale. She was sure that her friend Salvador would win.

On September 4, 1970, the house and telephone were at the disposal of the Movement of the Revolutionary Left. The main leaders of the group, Andrés Pascal, Miguel Henríquez, Juan Bautista von Schowen, and Carmen and Cristián Castillo were friends with Mabel Piccini and Carlos Sempat. Delia was unaware of this, but since their arrival she'd shared long conversations with them. She'd found them to be nice young people, pleasant, educated. So when they asked her if they could use her house to protect the popular triumph, she accepted without hesitation.

They settled into a room next to their bedroom. All day long there was a parade of people waiting for the television, the radio messages, the telephone calls that would let them know. At the moment of the victory, Delia cried and jumped up, forgetting her disability. There were drinks and champagne. Everyone stayed, keeping alert until dawn. In the midst of the commotion, on television they watched Allende arrive at the Alameda, get down from his mini red Austin and climb the steps of the Student Federation. The crowd overflowed into the street and squeezed together on the staircases of the National Library. The speech from a balcony by the victorious candidate, transmitted through worn-out speakers, could barely be heard.

Delia kept crying: "Salvador had to win, his cause is just, our cause is just…" and repeated a string of her Marxist-Leninist principles. "I'll never forget her joy," said Mabel Piccini.

The celebrations lasted several days. Delia sent telegrams of congratulations to Allende, to future ministers, to everyone. She was attached to the television, listening to all the broadcasts, reading *El Mercurio* meticulously, getting up late and looking for people in the house to point out the dangerous lines and sinister intentions that appeared in the newspaper.

With great difficulty, with pain in her legs, she kept working on her drawings, always waiting for a future exhibition. She worried about who would buy her works, her prints, because despite the hardships with money, she didn't want just anyone to have her things. At the same time, she gave things away, because nothing made her happier than for someone to be delighted by one of her works. "Let me give it to you, my son," she'd say, and add an original, eloquent dedication. While friends were making efforts on her behalf, she offered as gifts not only her works but things from the house, old memories. "Take it, my son, I don't need it."

During that time the lands in San Juan were sold. It wasn't much money, not even a shadow of what she'd invested. Someone advised a fixed-term deposit at the Central Bank. Many believe this deposit still exists. Perhaps she forgot it, or it was lost in her confusing system of diversifying information, saying certain things and concealing others.

Many of her friends received positions in the Allende government, jobs that demanded an enormous amount of time. Everything had been rocked by the election, even the smallest areas of daily life. So it happens that this period, with all its urgency, was somewhat more solitary for Delia. Nobody could give as much as she demanded. She understood this well, and continued to send telegrams to whoever appeared in the newspaper. She no longer had a huge group of people near her with time to spare, but on Fridays she continued the ceremony of her meal with friends, to which new people were always added, like the ambassador from France or the wife of the ambassador from Romania, who always brought an eggplant stew that had its supporters and detractors.

During one of these meals, Roser Bru brought a surprise. In a book of the complete poetry of Miguel Hernández, she'd discovered a poem dedicated to Delia, unknown to her. She read it out in front of all the guests.

Inventory that I dedicate to my friend Delia

What gentleness of a stroked lily / with your delicacy of washerwomen or objects of crystal, / Delia, with your waist made to be circled by a ring / with the most handsome stalks of fennel / Delia, she of the leg built with pursued hares / Delia, she of the open-mouthed eyes / of the same gesture and grace as young oxen. / In your tenderness the buds find their origin, / your tenderness is capable of embracing the thistles / and in her I see waters that pass and do not alter their course / between fierce shores of bramble and bull-fighting. / Your head of a sprig of grain sways to the sides / with a fainting of gold tired of abundance / and rises up flashing wheat in every direction. / You have for a tongue concentrated grape syrups, for lips balanced velvets, / your voice passes through a mineral cluster / and once a year through a sweet but irritable hive. / You will not find Delia except very spread out / like the bread of the poor / behind a kissable window: her smile / wanting to soothe the rage of fire, / tame the rustic soul of the horseshoe and flint. / There you are breathing feathers like the nests / and offering a few fingers of affectionate wool.

The poem was celebrated, analyzed, repeated. Delia was happy and sad. She remembered the times in Spain, and the outings with Miguel, when he'd climb the trees imitating birdsong. After that day, the poem was recited many times. Its reading was inevitable at gatherings.

The Lynch house was a box of surprises.

In January 1971, the English ambassador Geoffrey Jackson was kidnapped in Montevideo by the Tupamaros. For months no agreement was reached, and the ambassador remained in captivity. In July, the English ambassador in Chile and the representatives of the Uruguayan movement agreed to a conversation. The Mir was responsible for making arrangements. They needed to talk in a safe location. Delia's house was perfect. But they needed an appropriate occasion, some other event that would distract attention so the delicate conversation could take place. As if fallen from the sky came Delia's announcement to Mabel Piccini: "My daughter, the Moscow circus is coming. You know that artists always come to visit me; we have to prepare the party." Some eighty to one hundred artists would attend, exactly what was needed.

That Sunday, the party began at noon. The conversation was fixed for two in the afternoon. The ambassador in Chile, David Henry Thoroton, was escorted to the meeting place. He arrived when the party was at its peak. In the garden was a crowd including more than eighty Russians with trained dogs and monkeys, doing somersaults and showing off with juggling and contortion acts, encouraging each other with shouts and songs. The vodka they'd brought in boxes flowed. Nobody would have been able to notice the other occasion.

The ambassador was led to the second floor, where representatives of the Tupamaros and leaders of the Mir were waiting for him. They offered him vodka; he preferred whisky. The conversation lasted for over two hours, while outside, the euphoria increased in a confusion of toasts, accordion music and cries, as neighbors observed from the street.

"What are you doing up there? Come to the party," said the Ant, without knowing what was happening.

"Let me introduce you to an English friend," said Mabel, at the moment the ambassador was leaving. Delia spoke to him in English, and he kissed her hand as he said goodbye.

"You should invite your friend again, he's very pleasant." Delia was a passive accomplice. She wasn't deceived, but she didn't want to get involved. "I greatly respect all of you, you risk your skin. I don't share any of that, but I respect you."

The meeting worked. On September 7, one hundred and six Tupamaros escaped through tunnels from the prison of Punta Carretas. "Only with a corruption of the highest degree could these things have happened," the Defense Minister of Uruguay declared. Three days later, on September 10, after eight months of captivity, the ambassador Geoffrey Jackson was liberated in front of the Church of Saint Francis of Assisi, in the Nueva París neighborhood in Montevideo. After this, President Pacheco Areco entrusted the leadership of the anti-subversive struggle to the military authorities of the Army, Navy and Air Force.

At the end of the year, Delia went to Buenos Aires again to exhibit her paintings, this time at the important gallery Carmen Waugh had opened on Florida Street. For the catalogue, Emilio Ellena wrote to Rafael Alberti, who was living in Italy, to ask for a text.

My dear and often thought-of friend Ellena: this is my small homage to Delia, who would have wished for something more important. During the summer I don't live in Rome, so I receive letters with delay. But how could I not write something, even if it's short, for our adored and very beloved Delia. I hope it arrives in time. Send me a few words as soon as you receive this. Infinite thanks for having thought of me, of us. Write to me at Via Roma 46, Lazio. Or Via Garibaldi 2, Rome…

Delia Delia in the happiest days of Spain / Delia in the sad days and clearings of war, / Delia touched always with grace, / Delia always so beautiful / and slender, and Delia flower of unique unbending stem / Delia yesterday / Delia today / in our hearts as we stand astonished / at the youthful wind of your hair / lifting you, Delia, oh Delia, to the peaks / carried by the breeze / of your bold flurried hand.

Rafael Alberti. Rome, September 1971.

Once again many friends went to the inauguration, including María Teresa Sola, Carlos Lohlé, Marcela Sola, María Rosa Oliver, Victoria Ocampo, Raquel Palomeque, Horacio Coppola, Marina López and Bernardo Kordon. The Museum of Fine Arts in Buenos Aires bought a few works from her. But the consecration she'd hoped for didn't happen.

In October 1971, Pablo Neruda won the Nobel Prize in Literature.

"It seemed very natural to me," Delia said during an interview, the first in which she referred to herself and Neruda. "I admire his poetry very much, especially the *Canto General*, which a great Spanish poet called a Bible."

She added: "But I don't think he got the Nobel Prize because of his verses for Matilde Urrutia."

What did she think about Matilde Urrutia?

"I don't have an opinion about that person... neither dislike, nor affection. She made Pablo's sister and Homero Arce, his secretary, suffer very much... I suspect that some of these things brought on Laurita's death..."

Months later, Maruja Vargas de Mori showed up at her house, along with some friends of hers who wanted to buy prints. They went into the bedroom and there was Delia lying in bed, absorbed in the television.

"Do you mind if we finish watching this?"

On the small Antu TV she attentively watched the poet in his moment of glory, receiving the prize and afterward arriving at the Santiago airport with Matilde, to an enthusiastic reception.

At the end of the broadcast, she made no comment, pointing them toward a folder of prints they could choose from.

It was increasingly hard for her to settle herself in front of the easel, and almost impossible to climb a small ladder to finish the ears of an enormous horse. Her pains wouldn't leave her in peace. She decided to go under the knife again, since Doctor Croquevielle had assured her that a prosthesis was the perfect solution.

"What I want is to be able to paint and dance again. That's why I'm being operated on," she told friends, who were anxious because of her age. They feared she wouldn't make it.

But she went ahead with the procedure. Although she still had to use walking sticks, her mobility noticeably improved, and her pains disappeared.

She was able to travel to Montevideo to exhibit at the Uruguayan Soviet Cultural Institute, directed by her friend Silvia Mainero. The Chilean Embassy transferred her works there, and she stayed at the invitation of the ambassador.

The situation in Chile became chaotic. 1971 had seemed like progress, because despite the clamor of the opposition, there had been noticeable economic improvements for the popular classes, which gained access to opportunities that had been restricted. As the months passed, however, the specter of illegality and the regime's trajectory toward authoritarian communism were wielded by the right to justify a reaction against government policies, which seized industries, lands and fields in a nationalization of the means of production. After mutual betrayals and slander, the positions became irreconcilable. The only possible outcome was the defeat of the opponent. Shortages and the hoarding of goods brought the struggle to daily life, involving all citizens and winning new supporters to both sides, which were ever more unwilling to compromise. In this way, politics invaded the heart of the family and the workplace. The division extended to everything and everyone. The right-wing and Christian Democrat opposition adopted the tools of the popular struggle: mass marches, managerial strikes. The sum of events seemed to be weighed on an imaginary balance, alternating between periods that favored the government and periods that tilted toward the opposition, in segments of time that increased in intensity even as they grew more brief, confused and riddled with suspicions.

On the night of September 10, Belela Herrera, the wife of the Uruguayan ambassador and a friend of Delia's—Delia had known her father Carlos Herrera in Paris as part of the group close to Figari—went to pick her up for a party at the Bulgarian Embassy. Delia excused herself, as she felt tired.

Just like she did early in the mornings, she turned on the radio. The military marches every station was transmitting confirmed what had been suspected for months. All of a sudden, changing the dial, there was the voice of Allende saying goodbye. She received two brief phone calls, and then the telephone was cut off without a dial tone. Mabel and Carlos ran to her bedroom, stunned. The predicted coup had been carried out. The military factions announced an immediate curfew and read out the names of people who needed to turn themselves in at the Ministry of Defense. They were all friends, acquaintances. There was no other news. Bewildered, they waited for something else to happen, a communiqué from the army, anything. Perhaps this was no more than bravado. Delia didn't want to believe in this reality. Things that didn't agree with what she thought or wished were unacceptable.

The Military Junta's appearance on television put an end to the speculation.

A thick silence fell over the city, broken only by the sound of airplanes.

In the hearth, paper burned as important documents were set on fire.

The events of the day gave rise to an overwhelming grief.

On Wednesday the 12th, the curfew was lifted for a few hours so people could return to their homes and stock up on provisions. The supermarkets were crammed with goods that hadn't been there two days before, at extremely low prices that had been fixed by the Allende government. There had been a plot to create a false shortage. But it was pointless to complain about this detail now, in the face of such disaster.

Surreptitious news of executions, arrests and raids reached Lynch. First came disbelief, the way to avoid falling into panic. Then came the preventive measures, like taking shelter. The house was vulnerable. Mabel Piccini and Carlos Sempat left on Wednesday; so did the young people who rented out the other rooms. A few friends arrived to help the Ant and bring her food, and then she was alone with the maids.

The next morning, soldiers came. They surrounded the garden and fanned out at the entrances, preparing for a raid. She was in bed when they entered her room.

"Do you know this person?" they asked her, holding up a photograph.

"Of course I know him, that's Cristiancito."

They were looking for Cristián Castillo.

The house was thoroughly searched. Drawers were opened; the floor was torn up to check for weapons; the "lose-its", as Neruda had called the closets, were turned upside-down; and the garden was uprooted. Hundreds of books, the complete library of Carlos Sempat, were burned on the terrace.

The house was raided six more times over the next few days. Military officials were looking for several people who'd lived there.

"Do you know that every day I wake up with a soldier sitting on the bed?" asked Delia. She wasn't complaining. She knew what was happening in other places.

"Since you're tall, why don't you fix the curtain for me?" she asked a soldier, who was searching her drawers for the umpteenth time.

"Let's see, Mr. Official, what do you think, does this horse jump or not?" she asked, pointing to a drawing she was working on.

She wasn't afraid. She told the soldiers her opinions about everything they were doing in the country.

"I'm sorry, I'm leaving. I've been invited to lunch, and it's very hard for me to walk. I'm not going to come back to my bedroom and wait for you to do what you've got to do," she said.

On September 24, she learned of the death of Pablo Neruda.

The friends who went to see her found her sitting on the bed, crying.

"Did he ever love me? What would I have been without Pablo?" she asked Inés Valenzuela.

Despite the dangers, Mabel Piccini went to visit her. Delia was watching television. As always, her eyes were painted, and she was wearing a lot of mascara and powder. Tears rolled down her cheeks.

"Have you seen? Pablo died."

Belela Herrera offered to take her to the wake. Everything was arranged. But she didn't want to go.

"We've already created too much of a circus around the subject," she said to Emilio Ellena.

She read old papers. She hung a photograph over her bed, which showed her with Pablo and Gabriela Mistral.

Someone told her that Neruda's house had been raided too, that the plumbing had been broken, that water had run through the patio and garden, that people had gone to the wake and waded through the flood.

Pablo's death allowed her to remember him, to talk about him, to ask questions about his death and funeral. To cry over him in front of her friends.

Everyone close to Delia was so unsettled that they decided to take her to a calmer place, where she'd be better looked after, so she wouldn't have to endure the humiliation of the raids and the uncertainty about what might happen next.

They chose the house of Amoldo de Hoyos, a Mexican professor and friend of Emilio's. It was a spacious home, comfortable and safe, in the Providencia neighborhood.

But after two days there, Delia became completely paralyzed. After visiting, Doctor Paz Rojas, the daughter of Manuel Rojas, decided to hospitalize her.

She stayed at the José Joaquín Aguirre Hospital for almost two months. There had been a collapse of the vertebrae. Recovery was possible because the spinal marrow hadn't been affected. It was another stage of her advanced osteoporosis.

The loneliness of the hospital room drove her to despair. She talked with the trees outside the window. She sent messages, inventing urgent errands for Emilio Ellena—a spoon, eau de cologne. Doctors Erika and Pedro Castillo fulfilled her requests. Inevitably they were captivated by Delia's charm.

Coming back to the house gave her joy. It also gave her friends an enormous amount of work and worry. Everything had changed. The September coup had turned the world upside-down. It was hard now to find renters for the house. The friends the Ant asked about had become refugees, prisoners, illegals, exiles, missing persons and corpses. Goodbyes came from those who had managed to escape.

"We're leaving for Germany," Aída Figueroa told her. "Sergio got hold of tickets."

Delia sighed and her eyes filled with tears.

Amalia Chaigneau, to Mexico. Mabel Piccini and Carlos Sempat, to Mexico. Joan Morrison, to Sweden. José Balmes and Gracia Barrios, to France. One after another, her friends were leaving.

THE ANT

Some still gathered on Fridays. The dark house was lit up, food was brought out, pisco sours were poured. Roser Bru, Eduardo Vilches, Alicia Vega, Erika and Pedro Castillo, Belela Herrera and Emilio Ellena came. This was the only time when Delia left her bedroom. It took hours for her to get ready. She refused the use of the wheelchair. They helped her walk into the living room, but she insisted on concealing the help, pretending she could do it alone. In the back room, next to the fireplace, the dining table was set. There were few people there, but everyone listened as if for the first time to the memories of Spain, Federico, Miguel, Pablo. Someone recited Miguel's verses for Delia. And everyone left in a hurry—the curfew began at eleven.

The Ant's economic situation was precarious. Her bills required more than the occasional sale of prints, the help of friends or the monthly income sent to her by Matilde Urrutia through the Neruda Foundation. Of course Delia wasn't aware of this; she thought the money came from the sale of her works. Ramón González worked hard to find new renters, tracking them down among people who could be trusted in uncertain times. Daughters of old friends, music students, professors. Carmen and Daniel Pantoja. Sometimes, on Fridays, she would sit at the table with them after her friends had been forced home by the curfew. She didn't like to sleep early, but going out was impossible. These young people were moved by the stories of Spain that the Ant always told with some twist, some new detail. In this way, her house recovered some life.

Always concerned for her friends, she made inquiries with Belela Herrera, who helped transfer people to embassies with support from the United Nations. Miria Contreras was in danger, and when Delia's help was requested for a risky maneuver, she didn't hesitate. The plan was to go to lunch at the Argentine

Embassy with her nephew José Vicente del Carril, the Chargé d'Affaires, who had replaced the ambassador after the military coup. They'd use Belela's car, and Miria Contreras would come with them and slip into the embassy. But overnight, the civil servants who'd been informed of the plan and served as liaisons were transferred to Buenos Aires. The plan fell apart the day before it was carried out. Furious, Delia spoke harshly with her aunt over the phone, chastising her because she'd been responsible for the transfer of the civil servants.

In those first perilous years of the dictatorship, the opposition felt intimidated. Whenever they went out into the street, military squads in combat outfits holding machine guns emphasized the new reality.

All the same, small bastions of expressiveness slowly emerged. One of these was the Visual Arts Workshop at Bellavista Gallery, founded under the wing of the Archbishop of Santiago's Pro Peace Committee by Virginia Errázuriz, Francisco Brugnoli and Pedro Millar. Some of the students who had been dismissed from the arts faculty at the University of Chile worked there. Part of its funding came from the sale of prints; Roser Bru and Delia were the first to contribute pieces.

They brought a small stone to Delia's house to make lithographs. It was the first time she'd made one, but she drew a horse with grease pencil and took a confident step into the new medium.

She also made new editions on her old metal presses, with just two or three copies. Only a few people knew about the workshop. Sales were carried out in the presence of international officials.

In 1975, Delia exhibited her drawings at the Bellavista Gallery. Despite the circumstances, attendance was high, since it was the only way to stay in touch. Delia was in a wheelchair. All of a sudden, a man came up to kiss her.

She recognized his voice. "What are you doing here? Leave this place immediately."

The man looked at her, horrified. Despite changes to his hair and his appearance, she had identified him. He was Fernando Ortiz, leader of the Communist Party in hiding. He had lived at Lynch for a time, and Delia cared about him a great deal. But she thought at once of the danger he was in, and the risk to the lives of the others who were there.

Despite her disabilities, Delia insisted on going to Bogotá at the end of 1975 for an exhibition of her work. The Cultural Attaché of the United States Embassy in Chile, Frances Coughlin, had bought a collection of her prints, and she lent them to this show, which was organized by the Institute of Culture and the Center for Contemporary Art. Delia decided she must be present. Emilio Ellena accompanied her for a few days to Bogotá, and the trip also brought her to Lima, where Coughlin had been assigned.

The catalog of the fifty-one prints in the show included a text by Victoria Ocampo, written especially for the occasion.

> Delia and I get along wonderfully. Of course we do. It would be hard not to get along with her. Her ease for striking up a conversation with people of any age or sex, her natural affability, her wish to please humankind and her quickness in achieving it (helped by a dose of physical charm that nobody can overlook) have always been very outstanding gifts in her... These horses drawn by Delia, which rear up with spirit, just as in the pasture where they would have grazed, crowding together, waiting for the hour when the gate would be opened for them, are symbolic. Delia, with seeming ease, has managed to free them from their enclosure. None of this, however, was easy... We've defended, each of us in our way, and to the end, some noble illusions, and perhaps some generous errors. We've learned,

even so, to be friends, as well as citizens of a world where one doesn't stumble against borders, because they don't reach to the areas that matter.

This trip was full of marvels, of "miracles" as Delia liked to say. She hardly noticed the parade of friends, and friends of friends, who were prepared to help her into and out of planes, accompany her with paperwork, and go with her to all the places she wanted to visit, without obligation, enveloping her in an extraordinary affection.

The Argentine editor Carlos Lohlé was enthusiastic about Enrique Lihn's idea for a book of conversations with Delia. He wrote to her to persuade her to accept, saying he could publish it in the "Cuadernos Latinoamericanos" collection, and that he'd help her overcome her fear of talking to a machine. A similar book of conversations with María Rosa Oliver had already appeared. When Delia's consent came, Enrique began with enthusiasm, recording several tapes in addition to reading the letters of Neruda that she lent him. These readings inspired him to give a twist to the book. He wrote to Lohlé telling him that after what he'd found in the letters, it seemed important to concentrate on the Ant's poetic help with Pablo's poems.

But nothing happened. Some time later, the letters disappeared from Delia's house. The appropriate police reports were filed, but everything was left shrouded in mystery. All that remains of Enrique's work is the correspondence with the Argentine editor. There is no trace of the tapes or letters.

Without losing any energy, Delia was feeling the effects of the years, and she adapted to old age almost unconsciously. "People don't pronounce their words well anymore, I don't understand them," was her take on the deafness descending on her. Her immobility didn't lead her to distance herself from her favorite places, gallery openings or restaurants, where there was always someone to come with her. She found the food tasteless: "They don't cook well anymore."

For many years she'd been forgetting names. "Love," she'd say to everyone. She'd strike up the most natural and enthusiastic conversation and then ask: "Who was that charming person, my son?"

The only thing that made her despair was the lack of mobility that prevented her from advancing in her work. Bruno Tardito, a young art student, became her assistant in 1977. She would make the first strokes of a drawing, and then he would try to interpret her instructions. It was a laborious task that required hours of concentration to produce the exact thing she had in mind. After throwing tantrums when he didn't achieve something she considered to be incredibly easy, the Ant would congratulate him heartily when he managed it. Between arguments and affection, they managed to finish a gigantic work in a month.

Bruno remembers Delia's ninety-third birthday party. That night, inspired by joy, she'd danced a cueca with the poet Juvencio Valle. She took a few steps, waving the handkerchief, determined to defy her immobility.

But she was resisting the inevitable. With friends, she avoided revealing her total dependence on her maid and the nurse who looked after her. When someone came to visit, she demanded that they stay for a long time—"but not out of obligation"—and asked her helpers to bring lunch and serve tea: "You'll do it so well for me, my daughter, you do it."

Afraid of ending up alone, she used ruses to ensure she had company. Virginia Errázuriz visited occasionally to have new prints from the workshop signed. "No my daughter, today we're going to talk, it's been so long since we've talked. Come another day and I'll sign them for you."

This is why Fridays were so important to her. She'd start to get ready in the morning, and would call her closest friends on the telephone to make sure they didn't forget.

One of her last outings was in 1980, to an exhibition of photographs at Neruda's house in Isla Negra, at the Chilean-French Institute of Culture.

"You're going to come with me," she instructed Virginia Errázuriz. "You won't move from my side for any reason."

It was a masterful performance. The Ant in her wheelchair arranged to be at the center of the gathering. She moved from one side of the room to the other, with everyone coming up to greet her; she unfurled her charming exuberance, dramatizing the character she'd always been. Commenting on Fernando Opazo's photos, she made some biting remarks about the interior of the house.

She knew, of course, that Matilde Urrutia was in the next room.

Years after the death of the poet, Delia talked about him as if he were alive. The old feelings persisted in her. Love, because she'd have stayed her whole life by his side. Resentment and sadness, too.

CHAPTER 12

1982–1989

In the beginning were the memories. Her parents and siblings appeared again, and she repeated their names, talking about the ranch and the first horse she rode at four years old. "What can have become of Adelina?" she asked many times. While she was lucid, her memory set traps for her. The past revived itself, coming back as reality, all jumbled together.

She stared at the garden for hours, absorbed. A sudden interruption could make her forget her memory, before she returned again to silence.

Struggling to remember, she got angry.

There were problems with the caretakers. In 1978 Dinora Doudschitzky brought Rosita Callejas to look after her. The mutual affection was instantaneous.

"We have to write everything down in a notebook," Rosita Callejas told her, when she saw how desperate Delia was about her slips of memory.

"You're crazy," came the reply.

At night, Delia forced her to learn English and French, repeating phrases, throwing a cushion at her when she didn't do it well. Rosita was like a sister.

Delia ate little. Served meat with rice or eggs, she'd make drawings on the plate, spreading the pieces with her fork without trying a bite. All she wanted was ice cream. Half a liter at lunch, half a liter at night. She liked the feel of the cold sliding down her throat. At teatime, there was toast with avocado, like always.

"Friends don't come anymore," she'd complain. She forgot about the visits, the excitement of Friday nights, when people would stay until morning.

She gave in to daydreams, where the dead like Miguel Hernández continued to live. "You should invite that young man who's a goatherd, he whistles so beautifully."

She lived her dreams as a reality. "Last night the horses came." But her gaze was still direct and precise.

"What a good-looking young man this is," she said, when someone showed her an old picture of Neruda.

While looking through her photographs, stacked in cardboard boxes, she took a pair of scissors and cut his image away from every one.

When Pedro Castillo decided to operate, she wasn't aware of the urgency. It was a serious complication of the gallbladder and biliary ducts. After the operation, she slept for fifteen days.

"I have to recover," she said. And she did.

In September 1984 she celebrated her one hundredth birthday. Friends brought her a cake, and she clapped. She was happy in her own world.

Months later a hemiplegia left her absent, quieter than before. For the next three years she would be fed through a

Delia, around 1970.

gastric tube. Sometimes she watched the life around her with an astonished gaze.

When friends from exile began to return, her reaction of happiness seemed to come from an imaginary space, a remote association or powerful refraction that still held some meaning for her. Often she didn't recognize them. Aída Figueroa she did, when she returned in 1982. Aída read her the poem that Miguel

Hernández had written for her. But she couldn't recognize Sergio Insunza, who was able to come back in 1986.

"Ant, don't you remember how much we care about each other, my love for you and yours for me?"

"Look at the stories this one is telling me... And what does the young man do?" she asked Aída Figueroa.

"He's a lawyer."

"How terrible."

"Darling Ant, I'm Irene Domínguez." Irene waved her hands. Delia smiled.

Joan Morrison repeated her name and made gestures, but there was no response.

Amalia Chaigneau came up and took her hands. Delia had shrunk to a little lump of white hair.

"*C'est inexorable*," murmured Delia, speaking in French.

The dictatorship which had darkened her final years was reaching its end. Near her bed someone hung a sign for the "NO" campaign against the government. The opposition relentlessly hounded her with protests when it attempted a final maneuver to legitimize its power.

Delia survived long enough to protect her beloved house. The property had been expropriated by the military government, along with all the assets of the political parties. Only her death was necessary to seize it. Police officers had already come to take measurements of the garden, where they planned to dig a pool for themselves. This didn't happen, and after Delia's death the Communist Party was able to take back control of the house.

Early in the morning on July 26, 1989, after a calm night, Delia looked for Rosita with her eyes. Rosita held the Ant; Delia leaned her head against her, and after a short time, without complaint, she stopped breathing.

THE ANT

They held a wake in the old dining room. Rain was pouring down, and big drops fell from the roof onto the coffin.

"The drop of water that we are—which might be lovely for a moment—cannot be compared with the ocean. The important thing is the ocean. How can one believe that the soul is going to live when the continent of the human body disappears? The soul spills out like water from a flask when it breaks," Delia had said.

There was no fear in these words spoken in the last years of her life: a life whose length was perhaps a compensation for so many of its circumstances being out of phase, a life whose constant play of will and distraction found its harmony in her charm.

List of Interviews

In Buenos Aires: Margarita Aguirre, Esmeralda Almonacid Güiraldes, Blanca Isabel Alvarez de Toledo Bombal, Teresa Bortagarai Oliver, Horacio Coppola, Ángel Vergara del Carril, Conrado del Carril Videla Dorna, Teresa del Carril Videla Dorna, Alberto G. Lecot, Sara Jorge, Bernardo Kordon, Marina López, Samy Oliver, Raquel Palomeque, Eduardo Paz Leston, Juan José Sebreli, María Teresa Sola, Marcela Sola.

In Mexico City: Andrés Henestrosa, Mabel Piccini.

In Montevideo: Santiago Aguirre, Graciela Álvarez, Marta Amunátegui, Lavinia Andrade, José Balmes, Gracia Barrios, Jorge Bellet, Roser Bru, Elena Caffarena, Rosita Callejas, Mario Carreño, Leopoldo Castedo, Pedro Castillo, Amalia Chaigneau, Miria Contreras, Adolfo Couve, Poli Délano, Gabriel del Carril Amunátegui, Irene Domínguez, Luz Donoso, Jorge Edwards, Emilio Ellena, Virginia Errázuriz, Justa Espeleta, Irma Falcón, Lola Falcón, Aída Figueroa, Juan García Huidobro, Ida González, Belela Herrera, Sergio Insunza, Ramiro Insunza, Emma Jauch, Arturo Lorenzo, Sylvia Mainero, Fernan Meza, Pedro Millar, Joan Morrison, Marta Orrego, Sonia Ortega, Jorge Palacios, Daniel

Pantoja, Víctor Pey, Antonia Ramos, Oscar Soriano, Bruno Tardito, Volodia Teitelboim, Eugenio Téllez, Inés Valenzuela, Maruja Vargas de Mori, Ana María Vergara, Jaime Vicuña, Eduardo Vilches, Carmen Waugh, Sergio Würth, Enrique Zañartu.

Sources

The following libraries, newspapers and magazines were consulted:

In Buenos Aires: Biblioteca del Congreso de la Nación, Biblioteca del Jockey Club, Biblioteca del Museo de la Ciudad de Buenos Aires, Diario El Nacional, Diario La Nación, Diario La Prensa, Revista Caras y Caretas, Revista Mundo Argentino, Revista Plus Ultra.

In Santiago: Biblioteca del Congreso Nacional, Biblioteca Nacional, Diario El Mercurio, Diario El Siglo, Diario La Tercera, El Diario Ilustrado, Museo de Bellas Artes, Revista Apsi, Revista Hechos Mundiales, Revista Paula.

Interviews with Delia del Carril conducted by Magdalena Correa, María Teresa Diez, Jorge Marchant Lazcano and María Teresa Serrano.

Notebooks from the Fundación Pablo Neruda.

Exhibition catalogues by Delia del Carril.

Bibliography

Aguirre, Margarita. *Pablo Neruda, Héctor Eandi: correspondencia durante "Residencia en la tierra".* Editorial Sudamericana, Buenos Aires, 1980.

Alberti, Rafael. *La arboleda perdida.* Editorial Seix Barral, Barcelona, 1989.

Alone. *Historia personal de la literatura chilena.* Editorial Zig-Zag, Santiago de Chile, 1962.

Alfaro Siqueiros, David. *Me llamaban el Coronelazo.* Editorial Grijalbo, México, 1977.

Ayerza del Castilho, Laura and Felgine, Odile. *Victoria Ocampo, Intimidades de una visionaria.* Editorial Sudamericana, Buenos Aires, 1992.

Bordelois, Ivonne. *Genio y figura de Ricardo Güiraldes.* Editorial Universitaria de Buenos Aires, Argentina, 1966.

Clementi, Hebe. *María Rosa Oliver.* Editorial Planeta, Buenos Aires, 1992.

Délano, Luis Enrique. *Sobre todo Madrid.* Editorial Universitaria, Santiago de Chile, 1970.

Edwards, Jorge. *Adiós, poeta*. Editorial Tusquets, Santiago de Chile, 1990.

Finnamur, Jurema. *Pablo e dom Pablo*. Editorial Nórdica, Río de Janeiro, 1975.

Gibson, Ian. *Federico García Lorca*. Editorial Grijalbo, Barcelona, 1985.

G. Lecot, Alberto. *En "La Porteña" y con sus recuerdos*. Ediciones Rivolin Hnos. Buenos Aires, 1985.

Léger, Fernand. *Funciones de la pintura*. Ediciones Paidós, Barcelona, 1990.

León, María Teresa. *Memorias de la melancolía*. Editorial Losada, Buenos Aires, 1970.

Lottman, Herbert. *La rive gauche*. Editorial Tusquets, Barcelona, 1994.

Luna, Félix. *Historia de los argentinos*. Editorial Planeta, Buenos Aires, 1994.

Mayer, Doris. *Victoria Ocampo, contra viento y marea*. Editorial Sudamericana, Buenos Aires, 1981.

Morla Lynch, Carlos. *En España con Federico García Lorca*. Editorial Aguilar, Madrid, 1958.

Neruda, Pablo. *Confieso que he vivido. Memorias*, Editorial Seix Barral, Barcelona, 1974.

Neruda, Pablo. *Obras completas*. Editorial Losada, Buenos Aires, 1972.

Ocampo, Victoria. *Cartas a Angélica y otros*. Edición de Eduardo Paz Leston, Editorial Sudamericana, Buenos Aires, 1997.

Ocampo, Victoria. *Testimonios*. Editorial Sudamericana, Buenos Aires, 1946.

Oliver, María Rosa. *La vida cotidiana*. Editorial Sudamericana, Buenos Aires, 1969.

Ontañón, Santiago and Moreiro, José M. *Unos pocos amigos verdaderos*. Fundación Banco Exterior de España, Madrid, 1988.

Pastor Mellado, Justo. *La novela chilena del grabado*. Editorial Economías de Guerra, Santiago de Chile, 1995.

Penón, Agustín. *Diario de una búsqueda lorquiana*, 1955-56. Editorial Plaza & Janés, Barcelona, 1990.

Poniatowska, Elena. *Tinísima*. Editorial Era, México, 1992.

Sánchez, Luis Alberto. *Visto y vivido en Chile*. Editorial DESA, Lima, 1990.

Sánchez Vidal, Agustín. *Miguel Hernández, desamordazado y regresado*. Editorial Planeta, Barcelona, 1992.

Sarlo, Beatriz. *Una modernidad periférica. Buenos Aires 1920 y 1930*. Nueva Visión, Buenos Aires, 1988.

Sebreli, Juan José. *La saga de los Anchorena*. Editorial Sudamericana, Buenos Aires, 1985.

Sierra, Luis Adolfo. *La Historia del Tango. Osvaldo Fresedo*. Ediciones Corregidor, Buenos Aires, 1977.

Suárez, Eulogio. *Neruda Total*. Editorial América Morena, Chile, 1994.

Teitelboim, Volodia. *Neruda*. Ediciones Bat, Santiago de Chile, 1991.

Vázquez, María Esther. *Victoria Ocampo*. Editorial Planeta, Buenos Aires, 1992.

Acknowledgments

To write a biography is an impossible task if there are not many who are prepared to collaborate, listen, research along with the author and give him help. In this case, to confront the life of Delia del Carril was especially complicated. The life of the Ant stretched out over so many years, so many worlds.

First of all, I'd like to thank all the people I interviewed. I have indelible memories of every one of them. Thank you for your honesty, patience and openness. There were so many people had no reason to talk, but were eager to help, sharing with me their sense of an unresolved past and receiving me in their homes with an affection that gave me a sense of the strength, the transparency, the impact of Delia del Carril, who continues to exist in them, tremendously alive. I would especially like to thank Don Ángel Vergara del Carril, his wife, Susana Villamil, and their daughter María Isabel, who went far beyond courtesy and gave me essential information to begin the work, along with Paula Viale, who led me to them.

To Roser Bru, Emilio Ellena, Aída Figueroa, Sergio Insunza and Eduardo Vilches, for such displays of generosity and trust.

To so many of my friends who had to listen for so long to the stories about the Ant, and my ups and downs in the work;

to Delfina Guzmán, Pablo Núñez Gutiérrez, Alejandro Rogazy, Paz de Castro, Rosita Aguirre, Paula Andrade, and Juan Diego Montalva.

Impossible not to remember now, just like every day, Pilar and Pepe Donoso, still without having convinced myself that they are no more. We spoke about Delia for so many hours by telephone, in the garden, in the study, in the bedroom of that house belonging to Galvarino Gallardo, amidst the barking of dogs, the buzz of the doorbell. So many unforgettable moments.

To all those who collaborated with anecdotes, letters, information, photographs and contacts with the most disinterested kindness:

To Natalie Malinarich, Adriana del Piano, Andrea Lihn, Mena Bolton, Victoria Lago, Pablo Núñez Mardones, Felipe Sáez from Colombia, Jimena Pacheco, Jaime Vadell, Techi Edwards, Mónica Echeverría, Cristián Castillo, Sonia Ortega, Mark Falcoff, Patricia Israel, Carlos Cerda, Abraham Quesada, Blas López Caffarena, Francisco Javier Gamio, Michi Donoso, Aída Insunza, Paz Errázuriz, Pedro Valenzuela from the Embassy of Uruguay, Graciela Naon and Marcelo Giusto from the Argentine Embassy. To Ricardo Bravo, very especially. To Hildegarde Krassa and Carolina Briones from the Pablo Neruda Foundation. To Gian Bertolotto, who helped me with the notarial investigations about separations, and about the purchases and sales of the Ant's artworks. To Drina Beovic, for her concern.

In Mexico, to Jaime García Amaral, who has always received me with friendship in his home. To Justa Espeleta. To Mabel Piccini, for her trust and sincerity.

In Argentina, to Eduardo Ballester, whom I bothered so many times asking him for information, and who received me in his home. To Ricardo Seldes, who encouraged me when he read this book and also helped me to gather facts. To María Renée Rodrigué, Juan José Sebreli, Eduardo Paz Leston, Camilo Aldao and José Marcos Martín, for their information and kindness.

To Jessica Sequeira, for her marvelous work in translating the *hormiga* into an ant. To Brian Hurley and Michelle Lipinski, for their thoughtful and detailed editing.

To my brother Francisco, for his help with everything.

Index of Names